THE NEW MINNESOTANS

Stories of Immigrants and Refugees

THE NEW MINNESOTANS

Stories of Immigrants and Refugees

Gregg Aamot

SYREN BOOK COMPANY

MINNEAPOLIS

Most Syren Books are available at special quantity discounts for bulk purchases for sales promotions, premiums, fund-raising, and educational needs. For details, write

Syren Book Company
Special Sales Department
5120 Cedar Lake Road
Minneapolis, MN 55416

Published by
Syren Book Company
5120 Cedar Lake Road
Minneapolis, MN 55416

Printed in the United States of America on acid-free paper

ISBN-13: 978-0-929636-68-9
ISBN-10: 0-929636-68-6

LCCN 2006930596

Photo credits:
Bea VueBenson: AP photo stringer Janet Hostetter
Chong Thao: AP photo stringer Janet Hostetter
Omar Jamal: AP photographer Ann Heisenfelt
Ali Galaydh: AP photo stringer Andy King
Ahmed Wassie: AP photo stringer Dawn Villella
Gyuto Wheel of Dharma Monastery: AP photographer Jim Mone
Joselyn and Christino Casarez: AP photographer Ann Heisenfelt

Cover design by Kyle G. Hunter
Book design by Wendy Holdman

To order additional copies of this book see the form at the back of this book or go to www.itascabooks.com

CONTENTS

*For my parents
and for Jeanne*

FOREWORD

As this book is being published, an immigration debate is once again raging in many corners of the nation. Not unlike the widespread and vivid argumentation that played out in newspapers, pamphlets, and legislative chambers a century ago, we are deluged with a steady barrage of rhetoric either extolling the virtues of immigrant contributions to our economic well-being and cultural makeup or decrying the costs of meeting health care and educational needs of newcomers and their impact on social norms. Occupying center stage currently is the issue of how to address the reality of some 12 million unauthorized migrants already in the country with hundreds more arriving daily. Whether "legal" or "illegal," though, at the core of the immigration debate are always two questions: "Whom should we welcome?" and "How many?"

Minnesota is one of the states in which these questions are being asked and where immigration is at the forefront of public policy discussion. This would come as a surprise to most non-Minnesotans; indeed, even many in the state are perplexed about why this issue should be receiving persistent high-visibility attention in the media or on Capitol Hill. After all, Minnesota's overall foreign-born population is low compared to several other states of the coastal and southern border regions, as well as low compared to a century ago, when it had one of the nation's largest per capita immigrant populations.

But the face of Minnesota is unquestionably changing, and doing so much more rapidly than neighboring states. One of the key explanations for this is the state's well-established leadership in refugee resettlement. In 2005, the number of refugees received in Minnesota was surpassed by only that of California. This is not a contemporary anomaly but instead has historical roots stretching back to the immediate post–Vietnam War era and, in fact, even earlier to the post–World War II years. The legacy of this commitment has, over the past twenty-five years, brought about the extraordinary infusion of new Minnesotans described in greater detail in this book.

In addition to shining an appropriate spotlight on this evolving demographic and cultural landscape, Gregg Aamot's chronicle asks readers to consider the meaning and complexity of assimilation. Scholars, policy makers, and pundits have reached widely varying conclusions regarding the extent to which immigrants should and do assimilate within a dominant society. For many, the term itself embodies the notion of conformity, making it both an inaccurate and an undesirable conception of encounters between immigrants and mainstream culture. Recently, though, the analytical value of assimilation has been somewhat revived. That such assimilation happens, albeit on various levels and time frames, for different individuals and communities, is increasingly hard to deny. But what has become better appreciated today is the equal reality that assimilation is not unidirectional: the mainstream adapts to the immigrant as surely as the immigrant adapts to the mainstream.

A seasoned scholar of migration history once told me that the more she studied the immigrant experience, the more she realized there was no such thing as the immigrant experience. Perhaps more than anything else, the following pages underscore the validity of this point. While we can see some constants across time and among different cultural communities, immigration has always been an intensely human undertaking, and each individual story has something unique to tell us. I urge readers to resist the temptation to extrapolate too many generalities from the chapters that follow and use them to bolster a predetermined point of view in today's immigration debate. Instead, see these stories for what they are—the accounts of particular people in their own particular settings. After all, the ideal outcome of a series of human accounts like this isn't to sway opinion, it's to help us better understand our neighbors.

With the rise in immigration in Minnesota and the increasing attention from various quarters, it's a bit surprising that we don't yet have a comprehensive study of the topic, past or present. To be sure, the Minnesota Historical Society has published excellent monographs on various immigrant and refugee populations, superseding its earlier reference *They Chose Minnesota*. The University of Minnesota's Immigration History Research Center provides valuable, unique documentation on the state's immigrants. In recent years, studies produced by the League of Women Voters, the Wilder Foundation, Minnesota Advocates for Human Rights, HACER (Hispanic Advocacy and Community Empowerment through Research), the University of Minnesota's Center for Urban and Regional Affairs, the Hmong Cultural Center, the Minnesota State Demographic Center, and various other organizations have enriched our awareness of who has been settling in our state, why they do so, and what kinds of challenges they and their host society encounter.

But it has been especially the work of journalists throughout the state that has built the framework of information available to us on this evolving phenomenon. The best of these contributions have been features that go well beyond the headlines. Aamot's book takes us a step further—beyond the features. As such, it adds much-needed depth, reflection, and clarity at a time when all of these capacities and more are sorely needed in order to turn fractious debate into constructive dialogue.

Joel Wurl
Head of Research Collections and Associate Director
Immigration History Research Center
University of Minnesota

AUTHOR'S NOTE

I'm often asked about my job as a news service reporter. What is it, exactly, that I do? The simple answer is that I get paid to meet all kinds of people and learn their stories, write what they tell me, and then pray that it shows up in somebody's newspaper or broadcast. There's more to it, of course, but at the heart of it, that's what we reporters do. And it's not a bad job. The downside is that most of what we report has a shelf life of a day or two; then it's on to the next interview or event, recording the latest stories. And that often doesn't do justice to the culture-shaping stories that are an ongoing and important part of our lives, but also hard to think about in a coherent and meaningful way.

More than a decade in journalism has given me a front-row seat to a few of those stories, most notably the recent arrival of thousands of immigrants and refugees in Minnesota. I got an early start: As a cub reporter, some of my first assignments were writing about migrant workers who were putting down roots in my rural hometown of Willmar. I also wrote about expatriates living there who were fleeing the chaos of post-Soviet Russia. Later, after

I had joined the Associated Press, covering immigration put me in the homes and workplaces of Africans, Eastern Europeans, Asians, and others who found themselves, rather suddenly and sometimes inexplicably, living in America's Upper Midwest.

I had a lot of questions: What was life like for them? How were they adapting to their new surroundings? What did they think of Minnesota and Minnesotans? I began to tell the stories people shared, and doing so had the exciting feel of mapping uncharted territory. In some ways it was. Yet I also began to realize that I was, in other ways, simply telling familiar tales with different casts of characters. Not the same tales, but familiar ones. Minnesotans, to a degree and long ago, had been here before.

Immigrants, after all, had founded the state more than a century earlier. The historian William Lass, in his book *Minnesota: A History,* writes that immigrants arriving in Minnesota in the late nineteenth century were part of two movements: "westward movement within the United States and an international westward movement of Europeans to the United States." That massive wave of immigrants included—to name only some groups— Swedes, Norwegians, Danes, Germans, the Irish, Czechs, Slavs, Ukrainians, Belgians, and Finns.

By 1910, Lass reports, there were thirty-five identifiable ethnic groups on the Iron Range alone. Of this mixture, he concludes:

It is possible, of course, to single out particular ethnic contributions—the Germans to the art of brewing, the Danes to the development of the dairy co-operatives, the Scandinavians generally to education. But the greatest impact Minnesota's broad ethnic base has had may simply be that Minnesotans have a heightened awareness of the diversity that has created both Minnesota as a state and the nation as a whole.

Lass's book was published in 1976, generations after Europeans had decided to make Minnesota their home. As I read it two decades later, new immigrants and refugees were struggling to fit in. The wave of newcomers also seemed to be made up of two movements: from the southern United States and Mexico and—again westward—from Africa, parts of Asia, and Eastern Europe. And it included political refugees fleeing chaos and oppression, as well as immigrants who were leaving economic hardship for more opportunity. To Lass's list could now be added Koreans, Vietnamese, Mexicans, Colombians, Hmong, Somalis, Ethiopians, Russians, among others.

The melting pot metaphor is helpful in understanding ethnic and religious diversity and the positive and interesting contributions of new traditions in the United States. Yet in many ways, the established culture acts more like a strainer that filters the prejudices, beliefs, and customs of each new group. Some traditions and ways of life remain and thrive; others—often those that don't mesh with modern and democratic life—fade away.

The New Minnesotans: Stories of Immigrants and Refugees is about that cultural sieve and the people who are passing through it, balancing their heritage and traditions with life in another land.

The stories are an expansion of my reporting on several examples of that cultural tension. The first two focus on the Hmong and their struggle to overcome polygamy, as well as their work resettling a new generation of refugees. The third and fourth are about Somalis who are transcending clan loyalties and speaking out concerning their own welfare in Minnesota, and also working for the survival of their troubled homeland. The fifth story, meanwhile, tells of Ethiopians and their confrontation with social taboos in a race against AIDS, whereas the sixth focuses on Muslims from across the globe who are building their own religious communities among Minnesota's growing spiritual pluralism. Finally, the last story considers the largest group of newcomers, Latin Americans, and their efforts to preserve their identity while becoming an increasingly important part of the state's economy and culture.

The stories are laced with brief accounts of others dealing with assimilation, such as the Liberian and Burmese men who are speaking up for civil rights in their homelands while living in the diaspora in Minnesota, a Somali civic leader who is helping immigrant entrepreneurs start businesses, and the immigrant state employees who are teaching other newcomers about paying their taxes.

To set the stage, an introduction looks at the history of immigration in Minnesota and considers the parallels between the state's first newcomers and those moving here today. It also recounts my own awakening to this latest great migration—as a reporter observing the growing Hispanic influence in my hometown.

THE NEW MINNESOTANS

Stories of Immigrants and Refugees

INTRODUCTION

The stories in this book, and the challenges new immigrants and refugees are confronting in Minnesota, might be better understood after some historical reflection.

Minnesota was still a territory, home to Dakota and Ojibwe tribes and French fur traders, when the first great wave of immigrants began streaming across its borders. Scandinavians and Germans arrived first—in the largest numbers—followed after the Civil War by the Irish, English, Scots, Poles, Czechs, and a host of others. Many of them carved out their own settlements on Minnesota's prairies and along its rivers.

The newcomers were farmers and merchants and domestic servants, uprooted by agrarian crises in Europe and the uncertainties of the Industrial Revolution. Famine gripped Ireland. Unemployment swept across the Rhineland. Scandinavians felt the heavy hand of the state church. Meanwhile, an abundance of land was available west of the Mississippi River, and workers were needed in Minneapolis factories, on the railroad, and in the mines of the Iron Range. Some of the newcomers were simply old-stock Americans—Yankee pioneers from the Northeast—who were seeking fortune and adventure. Others were out to spread Protestantism in a new land. The West was opening up.

In 1860, New York governor William Seward, campaigning in Minnesota for presidential candidate Abraham Lincoln, reached out to the foreigners populating the young state. Seward, historian Theodore Blegen writes in *Minnesota: A History of the State,* considered the untapped West "a harmonizer of races, a region where the immigrants and their children became American citizens." Lincoln, his candidacy surely helped by such championing of these newcomers, easily carried the state in winning the election. Immigrants also fought to preserve the Union. Minnesota sent 24,000 men to the front lines of the Civil War, many of them fresh-faced recent arrivals from Norway, Sweden, Ireland, Germany, and other countries.

The race was on to populate the state. When the Civil War ended in 1865, there were 172,000 people living in Minnesota. By 1880, the population had swelled to more than 780,000, and 30 percent of them were foreign-born. Immigrants arrived in droves, enticed by stories—often embellished into myths and tall tales— about the benefits of the state's hearty climate and its abundant natural resources. Blegen notes that "Minnesota continued to welcome natives and foreigners" by pitching itself "as a Land of Canaan."

Civic leaders promoted the promise of Minnesota's vast southwestern farmlands, its thick woods to the north, and the fertile Red River Valley in the northwest. A Norwegian journalist named Paul Hjelm-Hansen worked as a publicist for the Red River Valley, writing articles for papers in both America and Norway. "I have made a journey, a real American pioneer trip, into the wilderness, with oxen and a farm wagon," he said in one article. "I have spent the nights in the open wagon with a buffalo hide as a mattress, a hundred-pound flour sack as a pillow, and, like Fritchof's Vikings, the blue sky as a tent." Thousands of Norwegians apparently endorsed his findings by settling in Minnesota.

Entrepreneurs saw the chance for riches. A Dutch businessman, Theodore Koch, exported Holstein cattle from Holland to Minnesota and bought hundreds of thousands of acres that he then sold to settlers. He founded several towns, including Clara City near my hometown of Willmar. Dutch pioneers had settled in Minnesota as early as the 1850s, and in 1868 the state issued a pamphlet in Dutch that promoted the virtues of Minnesota as a place to live.

Personal testimonials fueled the mass settlement. A Swedish immigrant, in a letter recounted by Lass, tells his family about the exhilaration of living in the new land:

No one need worry about my circumstances in America, because I am living on God's noble and free soil, neither am I a slave of others. On the contrary, I am my own master, like the other creatures of God. I have now been on American soil for two and a half years and I have not been compelled to pay a penny for the privilege of living. Neither is my cap worn out from lifting it in the presence of gentlemen. There is no class distinction here between high and low, rich and poor, no make-believe, no "title sickness" or artificial ceremonies, but everything is quiet and peaceful and everybody lives in peace and prosperity.

Minnesota was surely a more egalitarian place than the immigrants' homelands. But it was also segregated. Ethnic groups built their own settlements and published newspapers in their native languages. Churches were established along ethnic and denominational lines, and immigrants formed their own social clubs.

Swedes found the lakes region between the St. Croix and Mississippi Rivers, north of what is now the Twin Cities, to their liking. The Danes, on the other hand, settled in southern Minnesota, on the flat plains of Freeborn and Steele counties. The Dutch kept to a few pockets in the south and west-central regions, whereas the Czechs clustered near what is now New Prague and Silver Lake. Polish immigrants preferred the bustling cities of Minneapolis and St. Paul. These pioneers founded their own settlements and colonies and then worked to attract more of their own.

Newspapers were powerful tools for ethnic unity. Polish-language papers, for instance, "felt a sympathetic attachment to their kinsmen in Europe struggling gallantly for freedom and against oppression," Blegen writes. Similarly, native languages lived on for generations in the public schools. Czech teacher Antonin Jurka, for instance, taught his native tongue, as well as German, for several years in St. Paul. The adherence to language would last for decades. As late as 1925, according to a survey, 90 percent of the families in one Stearns County township spoke German in their homes.

The churches that dotted Minnesota's landscape symbolized the separateness across the state. Lutherans, Baptists, Methodists, Catholics, and others built churches that highlighted their particular languages and social customs. Norwegians resisted assimilation—especially religious ecumenism. Many immigrants considered themselves to be Norwegians—or Norwegian Lutherans—and thought of others as Americans. Herman Amberg Preus, in *The Religious Situation among Norwegians in America*, declared: "partly because of linguistic differences, but even more because of doctrinal differences, there can be no talk of the Norwegian joining or cooperating in ecclesiastical matters with his neighbors. He often has to live among American [sic] who have never been baptized and do not show the least interest in the church or the Word of God."

The Sokols, with their roots in nineteenth-century Bohemia, were places where Czechs gathered to socialize, dance, compete in gymnastics, and discuss the important issues of the day. The clubs fostered the Czech tradition of free thought and sometimes surpassed churches as the center of Czech communities. Germans founded the German Reading and Educational Society in St. Paul, ostensibly to spread enlightenment values. They built churches across the countryside, and German Lutherans fiercely protected their language and customs against what they considered secular encroachment.

Indeed, far from assimilating, these groups used their unique institutions to foster distinctiveness in a state growing in pluralism. According to Blegen, "Yankee, German, Norwegian, Swedish, Irish, Czech, Welsh and other settlements and 'colonies' that took root in the 1850s expanded and deepened 'in their special character' after the Civil War." That special character grew, creating a sense of cosmopolitanism in Minnesota and other parts of the Upper Midwest, and by the turn of the century, the state's population was nearing two million.

Powerful voices argued against assimilation. As late as the 1920s, O. E. Rölvaag, author of the famed immigrant novel *Giants in the Earth,* said Norwegian immigrants were "strangers to the people we forsook and strangers to the people we came to." Better, Rölvaag argued, to cling to ethnic differences as assimilation would lead to an empty society, a culture without substance that resembled a "gilded shell." Norwegian immigrants, rather than simply becoming Americans and absorbing the country's dominant culture, merged their old and new identities.

These early settlers passed through the cultural strainer, balancing their particular backgrounds and religious views with Minnesota's changing ethnic landscape. They feared that if they leaned too far in one direction, they might lose their most treasured traditions and ways of life. Lean too far in the other, and they risked perpetual isolation.

Some leaders, however, lobbied forcefully for unity. Georg Sverdrup, an Augsburg Seminary official, promoted public education as early as the 1870s, not long after the Civil War, saying it was necessary to help children "grow into the language and history of this country." The newly minted ethnic and religious colleges found a way for settlers to understand their varied European heritages while rallying around a common American purpose. People from different backgrounds also worked together, necessarily, to build the economy. The Irish, Scandinavians, and others provided the labor that built the state's railroads. Slovaks and other Eastern Europeans worked as loggers in northern Minnesota, in the flour mills of Minneapolis, and later in the deep taconite mines of the Iron Range.

As the nineteenth century turned into the twentieth, Minnesota grew in pluralism while maintaining its ethnic distinctions. This dichotomy became most evident during a dark chapter of World War I, when some residents—especially those of German descent—were the target of a state-sponsored loyalty campaign. In April 1917, soon after the United States entered the war, the state legislature created the Minnesota Commission of Public Safety. The name sounded like a law enforcement agency, and the commission officially was charged with maintaining public order and enhancing the state's contribution to the war effort. But it had a different mission.

As journalist D. J. Tice recounts in *Minnesota's Twentieth Century: Stories of Extraordinary Everyday People,* the commission used its authority to root out "disloyalty" and fight labor unionism and agrarian activism. It interrogated and intimidated Minnesotans who declined to buy the Liberty Bonds that helped finance the war. And it created the Scandinavian Press Service to monitor foreign-language newspapers. Tice writes: "In 1905, no less than 70 percent of Minnesotans were either foreign born or had foreign-born parents. Concern was widespread that newcomers might be less than wholeheartedly devoted to America's war aims or to its political and economic systems."

A particular target of criticism was the southern Minnesota city of New Ulm, home of the Hermann Monument, a statue depicting the Germanic tribal leader

Arminius, who defeated the Romans in about 9 A.D. The Minnesota Commission of Public Safety ousted New Ulm's mayor, Louis A. Fritsche, and its city attorney, Albert Pfaender, after both spoke at an antiwar rally and argued that men who opposed the war shouldn't have to be drafted into the military. (The two men persevered: Fritsche was later re-elected mayor while Pfaender became a University of Minnesota regent.) The commission also forced the board of Martin Luther College in New Ulm to suspend its president, who likewise had spoken at the rally.

Few immigrants came to Minnesota between the world wars, an era when the state's ethnic and religious distinctions lessened and began to meld. A handful arrived during the early years of the cold war, mostly political refugees from Communist takeovers in Czechoslovakia, Hungary, and elsewhere. But those post–World War II years set the stage for the wave of refugees who would begin arriving in Minnesota in the later decades of the century.

Churches became resettlement institutions, supplying the nuts and bolts of daily living, such as housing, clothing, furniture, and utensils. Eventually, they provided refugees with the know-how for tapping into government and charitable aid. Consequently, once the U.S. government let refugees into the country, it was often left to churches to step in and ease the transition. Lutheran

Social Services and Catholic Charities—representing the two largest religious denominations in Minnesota—were pioneers in refugee resettlement work.

In the 1970s, many Southeast Asians began coming to Minnesota, mostly refugees from the Vietnam War. A pair of bunk beds from my house went to a Willmar family that was taking in several of the "boat people" who had fled their country after the war, sometimes on makeshift rafts. But immigration was minimal compared with the turbulent decades after the state's founding a century earlier. It was a period when real rifts over religion, language, and cultural mores had long given way to the softer divisions of tradition and taste that lend Minnesota its particular ethnic flavor.

The current newcomers—East Africans, Southeast Asians, Mexicans, and Central Americans—began arriving in large numbers in the 1980s. They were also fleeing civil war and famine. They, too, came in search of jobs, equality, and adventure. And they brought with them another batch of new traditions, languages, and customs competing with the old. By then, Minnesota was well versed in adopting newcomers.

"Resettlement really changed and became formalized then because so many people were coming after the Vietnam War," explained Patti Hurd, director of Refugee and Employment Services for Lutheran Social Services. "Up until that time, churches were doing it informally, but it became overwhelming, and in the mid-

'70s the government began subcontracting the work to groups like ours." By the 1990s, Lutheran Social Services and Catholic Charities were among a handful of social services agencies in the country relocating refugees—hundreds or more each year in Minnesota alone. In 2005, Hurd and her staff helped more than 1,500 refugees settle in Minnesota—half of them Hmong, the other half Africans. It was the most refugees Lutheran Social Services had resettled in Minnesota in a single year since 1979.

As I write, demographers estimate there are 175,000 Latinos and Hispanics, 60,000 Hmong, 25,000 Somalis, and 25,000 Vietnamese in Minnesota. Leaders of these communities claim there are many more. Russian, Cambodian, and Ethiopian populations number in the thousands, as well. And there are other tiny populations of newcomers among Minnesota's five million people.

What forces encouraged these immigrants and refugees to come here? Experts point to three factors: a good economy with plentiful jobs in manufacturing and agriculture (such as the turkey processor in my hometown); a social services infrastructure that supports relocation (including not only religious-based groups but also new ethnic fraternal organizations); and, to a lesser extent, the opportunity—for people used to life in villages and remote outposts—for rural migration (into small Minnesota towns like Marshall, Worthington, and St. James).

"There's no real proof of this, but I think we have had congregations here that opened the door," Hurd said. "Going way back, we had a lot of immigrants, Germans and such, and congregations helped them. If people knew of someone needing help, they would call the church and say, 'We need help!' And it just perpetuated itself. But who knows for sure?"

While Yankees from the Northeast bypassed the Upper Midwest and headed for warmer climates farther south, my ancestors set down roots in Minnesota and North Dakota. A great-grandfather on my father's side homesteaded land in 1870 in western Minnesota, near what is now the Lac Qui Parle reservoir. An aunt and uncle live there now, next to a Lutheran church that was built in 1876. My paternal grandmother was also from a Norwegian family that settled in the same area of the state.

My grandfather on my mother's side, meanwhile, was a Dane who came to America in 1916 and eventually ran his own creamery in eastern North Dakota. (Lass, the historian, credits Danes for their contribution to the Upper Midwest's dairy industry.) His wife, my maternal grandmother, was born to Swedish settlers on a farm in northeastern North Dakota.

The pioneers in my family tree left the worlds they knew—the comfortable places of their families, friends, and traditions—and set out for new lives. It couldn't have been easy. The Minnesota author Bill Holm discusses this phenomenon in relating his craving for place, which he calls *from-ness*. Proud of his Icelandic ancestry, Holm returned to his hometown of Minneota in southwestern Minnesota after spending years in far-off cities and countries. In *The Heart can be Filled Anywhere on Earth,* he writes of his travels:

> I found life without *from-ness* too desiccated for my taste. The only people who interested me when I tried living anywhere else—the East, a city, Europe, even China—were either genuine natives still mired in their own *from-ness*, or true refugees and emigrants, driven from their first *from* by some twentieth-century necessity: war, starvation, political upheaval. Their lives left them no choice but amputation without anesthetic of the old *from,* thus the genuine necessity to invent a new one.

My great-great-grandparents came to Minnesota from Norway in old age and realized—too late to return—that they didn't really want to be here. Surely they found it painful to amputate their old *from.* Many clearly did. As many as 25 percent of the Norwegian immigrants to the United States eventually resettled in Norway. On the other hand, the Danes who moved here, more than most other immigrant groups, eagerly abandoned their native language in favor of English—and as a result quickly began to thrive.

The two-volume, multiauthor book *American Immigrant Cultures* characterizes Minnesota's immigrants in broad swaths. My ancestors, the Norwegians, for instance, are noted for their "values of thriftiness, environmental concerns, conservation of resources, hard work, simplicity, and quality of life issues." Such distinctions, though facile, add to an understanding of the state's culture and history, and similar descriptions will someday be attached to new immigrants and refugees.

Straightforward comparisons aren't easy to make, however. Roughly one million immigrants came to Minnesota between 1820 and 1950, and there are far fewer newcomers in the state today than there were 100 years ago. The 300,000 immigrants and refugees in Minnesota in 2005 made up 5.9 percent of the population. In 1910, the state had 550,000 immigrants who made up 29 percent of the population. Moreover, the state's earlier European immigrants were mostly white and Christian. Most also came from countries that were modernizing and, in most cases, experimenting with democracy.

Those similarities helped the various ethnic groups get along, even though language and denominational barriers initially divided them. "Compatibility of cultures has allowed assimilation to take place without negating heritage," the author in *American Immigrant Cultures* concludes about the Norwegians. "Rejection of heritage was not necessary for social acceptance into the mainstream society."

There were many reasons for the first great migration. Besides the availability of land and better jobs, Minnesota's first immigrants were fleeing a host of social and political ills. Europe in the eighteenth and early nineteenth centuries, while modernizing, remained a bastion of legal inequality, social stratification, and state-dictated religion. Immigrants hoped to escape those barriers and find something better in America.

Minnesota's new immigrants have faced similar obstacles in their homelands. The Communist government in Laos mistreated the Hmong. Ethiopians suffered severe famine. Civil war struck Somalia and Liberia. Mexicans worked for low wages. Yet, in other ways, the recent immigrants have far different backgrounds, ones that will be explored in this book. More than the first wave of immigrants, new immigrants and refugees face the painful prospect of rejecting those parts of their heritage that don't mesh with modern and open life.

I have always been interested in the immigrant experience. As a boy, I remember asking my grandfather to point out his Danish hometown on a map. For the subject of my senior thesis in college, I chose Oscar Handlin, a pre-eminent American historian of immigration. Later, I visited distant relatives in Denmark and Norway. But for years, my image of the immigrant was something from deep in the past: the romanticized, Ellis Island, European peasant version. I didn't pay much attention to new immigrants and refugees—or recognize the cyclical nature of American immigration—until they were all around me.

These newcomers first made an impression on me while I was doing something nowhere near romantic: walking through a dilapidated trailer park. Elm Lane sits abandoned now, on the edge of my hometown, grown over with grass, smooth and green. The trailers are gone. But not long ago, it was at the center of a contentious public debate that foreshadowed the challenges of new immigration.

The trailer park symbolized the growing Hispanic migration to rural Minnesota towns. It offered what those small towns needed: inexpensive housing for a growing Hispanic working class that provided low-cost labor for the local poultry-processing industry. But poor enforcement of laws and regulations, a wayward landlord, and tenant misbehavior conspired to make it a giant community headache. As one city leader who took me aside told me, when I was a reporter there and writing about the trailer park, "There are good things going on in this city, but this thing gets everybody's attention. It gets *your* attention. And it seems like that's all we're dealing with right now."

Migrant life began to change in the 1980s and early '90s. More and more seasonal workers—who happened to be mostly Hispanic Americans or Mexicans—had come to see Minnesota not simply as a temporary place to work and collect a check but as a good place to live and raise their families. Until then, they had been mostly invisible, drawing passing glances as they toiled in fields along the highway. For decades, Hispanics had traveled to the Upper Midwest from Texas and elsewhere in the Southwest, or from Mexico, to work in the fields and help farmers harvest their soybeans or sugar beets before returning home for the winter. Now they were coming to stay.

Hispanic boys and girls showed up at my elementary school on the north side of Willmar in the 1970s. My friends and I never really got to know these children; they would arrive in our classrooms one day, stay a month or two, and vanish. But by the late 1980s, more and more of these previously seasonal workers were putting down roots. They took unskilled but decent-paying jobs at poultry-processing plants and other businesses across western and southern Minnesota.

When I was in the sixth grade, approximately 200 Hispanics lived in Kandiyohi County. Fifteen years later, about 2,000 lived there, most of them in Willmar, the county seat. By some accounts in the mid-1990s, 10 percent or more of the city's population was Hispanic, and as many as a third of them were living in Elm Lane. In Minnesota as a whole, the Hispanic population grew 166 percent in the 1990s, rising to 143,000 by the turn of the century, or about 3 percent of the state's population. In the same period, the foreign-born population in Minnesota more than doubled, from 110,000 in 1990 to about 240,000 in 2000.

When I was growing up, Elm Lane was a neighborhood of white working-class families. Eventually, seasonal workers began renting or buying the trailers and told their families and friends back home about the neighborhood. It became a popular destination for migrants trying to start a new life. But after years of isolation from the rest of the town, it also turned into something no one anticipated: a barrio in the Upper Midwest. At its peak, more than 500 people lived there in 130 trailer homes. Seven or eight people lived in some of the cramped sixteen-footers. Weekends were like small festivals, complete with beer kegs, horseshoes, and loud Latin music. "I loved living there. It was a whole community," one Elm Lane resident, Martina Diaz, said after she and her family had moved out of the park and into a house in another Willmar neighborhood. "We are very happy people and lived like one big family— united. We fought just like any family, but most of our problems were caused by outsiders."

My editors at the *West Central Tribune* sent me into the park on story assignments—after reports of shootings or fights we'd heard about from the police or, on better days, in search of people whose stories might make an interesting profile. I roamed the park's dusty gravel streets one hot and humid August morning in 1994, the day after the funeral for Jesús Molina, who had been shot and killed after getting in the middle of a drunken brawl. I was looking for his wife and their seven children.

I found Connie Molina and her children—she had nine in all—living in one of the most rundown trailers in the park. The youngsters, some of them barefoot—the girls in skirts and the boys in dusty tank tops or sweatshirts—poured out of the trailer and crowded around their mother on the front steps. "He was stopping a fight," Connie Molina said through an interpreter. "I don't know what the fighting was all about, but a lot of it is because of drinking. People stay up till two or three in the morning partying."

As they sat somberly for a picture, I looked at the gravel roads crisscrossing the neighborhood and the paint peeling off the trailers. Jesús Molina was the fourth person to have been shot in the park in about a year's time. In one drive-by shooting, a man was wounded in the thigh while he and his five-year-old son, whose cheek was grazed by a bullet, watched television in their home. Another man was peppered in the buttocks with a shotgun. Elm Lane had become a world apart from the rest of the town. (It didn't help that the landlord, who lived near the Twin Cities, refused to adhere to a city ordinance designed to improve living conditions in the park by creating more space between homes. As it was, the park was so tightly packed that fire trucks couldn't drive on its narrow streets.)

As I left the trailer park after interviewing Connie Molina and drove toward the highway that led into the center of town, a group of teenagers walked in front of my car and surrounded it. Wads of spit landed on my windshield. "Get the hell out of here, gringo!" one of them shouted. After Molina's death and several fights that summer, the place was simmering, and I wasn't surprised at the teenagers' anger. Still, a gringo? In my hometown? I muttered a few unkind words and sped out of there.

The publicity made city leaders a little gun shy. Some of them blamed my newspaper for stoking tensions. Readers called to criticize my coverage of the shooting and other incidents in the park, calling me either a racist or a liberal agitator, depending on their point of view. The mayor at the time, Richard Hoglund, tried to help Hispanics feel welcome. In 1990, just as Hispanic migrants were beginning to make Willmar their permanent home, he formed a commission to look at race relations in the city.

The panel studied housing costs and how Hispanic students were treated in school, and it organized cultural festivals at which people shared food and music. About four years after Hoglund put his panel together, I asked him whether he thought it was really doing any good, and his response summed up the prevailing mood among the city establishment: "Part of the community is beginning to say, 'We've done this and we want to help the Hispanic community, but now it's time they meet us halfway,'" he said. "I think that's reasonable."

I left Willmar a few years later and eventually ended up with a job writing for the AP in Minneapolis. The Hispanic population grew to such strength in Minnesota that Mexico opened a consulate in St. Paul in the winter of 2004. Mexican president Vicente Fox even came for a visit. I forgot about Elm Lane, and soon after I left town tow trucks and bulldozers rolled into that neighborhood and erased a bleak moment in the city's history. I was glad to see it go, both for the people who had lived in near squalor there and for the city, which had become a target for critics. But pondering that ugly piece of real estate provided a glimpse into the difficult changes new immigration was bringing to Minnesota, and the challenges immigrants and refugees faced. My explorations led me to the following stories.

Bea VueBenson

AN ONGOING PROBLEM

The Hmong Face an Old Tradition

The Reverend Bea VueBenson walked briskly down a hallway at Gustavus Adolphus Lutheran Church in St. Paul, stopping to offer a quick handshake or hug before moving on. As a Hmong pastor at a mostly white church, her job was difficult and time-consuming enough: putting a Hmong face on a bastion of Minnesota traditionalism. But she had also taken on the more urgent task of mentoring teenage Hmong who were living between the pull of modern America, on one hand, and strict family bonds on the other.

VueBenson had been in the United States for twenty-five years. Born in Laos, she spent three years in a refugee camp in Thailand before her family moved to the United States when she was ten years old. After graduating from St. Olaf College and Luther Seminary, she became Gustavus Adolphus's conduit to the city's Hmong residents. That made her a prominent Christian in a community steeped in the Buddhism and animism of Laos. Even her last name—a hybrid that combined her own with that of her husband, a South Dakota native—suggested her comfort level with both worlds. (Hmong women, by tradition, usually retain their clan name when they marry.)

I met VueBenson at her church one fall afternoon in 2002. More than two decades had passed since Hmong refugees—among the flotsam of the Vietnam War—had begun fleeing Laos for the United States. Thousands ended up in Minnesota and Wisconsin, making the American Upper Midwest the unlikely heart of the Hmong diaspora. But Hmong students, most of them born in Minnesota, with no firsthand experience of Laos, faced dualities that would be difficult for any teenager. The clan ethos of their tight-knit families, for instance, stood in stark contrast to the individualism of American culture. And their religious traditions were competing with Minnesota's predominant Christianity. For a minister to Hmong youth, that made for a full plate.

At the time, VueBenson was dealing with one particular example of that cultural tension: Hmong men living in Minnesota were still taking second and third wives, a common and cherished practice in Laos. Second-generation Hmong—or those like VueBenson who had come to the United States when they were young—quietly fought the practice. They were reluctant to talk about it with reporters because of the stigma attached to it, yet angry at its resilience in America.

Like most people, I thought of polygamy as a bizarre and lingering offshoot of the Church of Jesus Christ of Latter-day Saints—the Mormon Church—practiced by religious zealots in the Utah backcountry. At their roots, however, such marriage arrangements are less about religion and more about patriarchal cultures, making them common in the third world. VueBenson wasn't sure she wanted to speak to me and complained that her comments about the issue in a recent TV news report had been taken out of context. But after a few minutes on the phone, she agreed to an interview.

I wasn't eager to write about polygamy. For one thing, I didn't know whether the practice was prevalent enough to warrant any coverage. What would be the point of writing about a few men who were clinging to an outdated lifestyle, if that was indeed the case?

And I tried to avoid stereotyping any group. By then, the Hmong image in the media was mixed. To be sure, many stories told of the journeys Hmong families had taken to get from Laos to the United States. More and more focused on the achievements of Hmong students or businesses. But some traditions and practices also came under scrutiny, such as slaughterhouses that failed to meet safety and sanitary codes and funerals that lasted for days, disrupting neighborhoods. Those were legitimate stories, but why add to them unless it was really necessary?

Polygamy, however, was happening on a larger scale

than I had thought. Young women, including some teenagers, were resisting the practice. It also held risks for
men because the practice could be grounds for the denial of citizenship. The debate was coming to a head,
and it showed just how difficult it was for some newcomers to strike a balance between their traditions and
accepted ways of life in America. The practice couldn't
be ignored.

As I reported on refugees, I would meet others like
VueBenson: educated and ambitious, fiercely loyal to
their native culture but willing to shed light on its dark-
est corners. VueBenson was outraged by the tales she
heard from teenagers about wayward fathers and the
second and third wives—and families—they kept across
town or on the other side of the neighborhood. She was
offended by the subservient role to which polygamy
subjected women and regretted the stigma it was leaving on the Hmong community.

"When I first got into the ministry and started working with these students, it was my impression that polygamy was on the decline. It's not legally and culturally
appropriate," she told me the afternoon we met at her
church. "But when I started working one-on-one, these
young people would tell me their stories, saying things
like, 'My dad doesn't live with me,' or, 'He lives with my
stepmom and comes over two or three times a week.'"
Some of the students wept as they told VueBenson their
stories. "I asked myself, 'Is this a coincidence, or does it

reflect a growing pattern?' I'm convinced it's part of a larger problem," she said.

The issue was mostly hidden and out of the reach of the mainstream media. That left the task to tiny ethnic publications. *FutureHmong*, an Appleton, Wisconsin, magazine, jumped into the fray. The magazine covered Hmong life and occasionally stuck its neck out on sensitive cultural issues. Blong Yang, the magazine's editor, was young and educated and walking a fine line between respect for Hmong culture and criticism of its patriarchy and clan structure. Yang's outspokenness alienated him from many Hmong in Appleton—and some readers— but he was fearless in challenging accepted ideas about polygamy. He talked to me openly about it, though he wouldn't give away the identity of any friends or family members who were practicing the old ways.

"If I was naming names, I could name forty to fifty people, just off the top of my head," he said on the telephone one afternoon. "It's an ongoing problem in the Hmong community that's kind of hush-hush. It's still practiced on a daily basis by Hmong elders, and it's starting to spill over to younger kids that are growing up in America." He added: "Look, there are people my age who are doing it. They won't talk to you about it. It's kept pretty secret, but it's happening."

Yang criticized the practice in an editorial in the March 2002 issue of *FutureHmong*. "There's a Hmong couple living in Wisconsin that is on the brink of divorce," he wrote. "Their family has been falling apart on all sides. Relatives have turned against each other. Some of the adult children have turned their backs on their parents for many reasons. This entire family is now broken and can't be repaired. One main reason is polygamy . . . the husband wanted to marry one more wife and the wife refused.

"In Appleton, another Hmong man gloats at a large family gathering and invites everyone to attend his second wife [sic] wedding," the editorial continued. "This man went around proudly with his head held high and chest out proclaiming he has became [sic] a true man by marrying two wives, not even thinking about the consequences of his actions." Yang concluded: "Polygamy is wrong and it destroys families here in America."

Yang was bombarded with e-mails—hundreds of them, he said—from angry Hmong men who defended the lifestyle. One reader, a twenty-four-year-old man who identified himself as Song, wrote: "When you make polygamy illegal, you take away people's rights . . . People who choose a polygamist lifestyle should not be ashamed, it is your right." The reader argued that since, as he mistakenly understood, gay marriage was legal in the United States, polygamy was simply another acceptable family structure outside the traditional nuclear kind. Yang laughed at such criticism, but there was frustration in his voice. "I'm glad my column created a lot of feedback, but as you can see, a lot of people need to be educated, and that takes time."

Blong Xiong had recently joined the faculty at the University of Minnesota when we met in his East Bank office. The walls were bare, and boxes of books remained unpacked on the floor. Xiong was a social sciences teacher in the General College, where students with modest high school records honed their study habits before entering one of the university's degree-granting colleges. He had researched Hmong family life for his doctoral dissertation and was eager to talk about polygamy and how it was spilling into his generation.

Xiong fled Laos with his family in 1980 and resettled in Minnesota in 1982, when he was fifteen years old, and graduated from Hastings High School on the southeastern edge of the Twin Cities. "I think the issue remains very constant with the first generation of immigrants," he said. "I don't see as many younger people engaged in polygamy—there is more egalitarianism rather than patriarchy in their relationships. There was a lot of talk about it among men my age when we came here, but not a lot of carrying it out."

Xiong came up with a best guess of the extent to which polygamy was being practiced in Minnesota after interviewing about three dozen families for his dissertation. Based on his understanding of clans and his discussions with those families, Xiong estimated that between 270 and 450 men were practicing polygamy in Minnesota (mostly in St. Paul, which, with an estimated 24,000 Hmong, had the largest Hmong population of any American city), each with an average of two wives and fourteen children. That translated into as many as 7,600 men, women, and children living in polygamous families.

When I told him that seemed like a lot, he shrugged his shoulders and smiled, as if to agree. "I don't know if people are getting smarter about it or whether it's becoming more informal, but I know it's happening," he declared. Whether the practice of polygamy was taking on different forms was less important to Xiong than the fact that it still existed and reinforced patriarchy in the culture. He wanted to conduct research on the subject, even though he knew it would mean stepping on some toes in his family and social circles. "My interest is in finding out if these relationships are still formalized, or if they're informal, like having a mistress, which would still have an effect on children," he said.

By some estimates, there were as many as sixty thousand Hmong living in Minnesota by the turn of the twenty-first century. When they first started arriving in Minnesota in the late 1970s—most of them settling in St. Paul—most people had no idea about their background as U.S. allies during the Vietnam War. To many

Minnesotans, they were simply refugees for some reason or another. "Are they Korean or Vietnamese?" I was once asked. Some people believed they lived in clans or were part of a cult. And so on. I didn't know much about them at first, either. It was clear, though, that like many new immigrants and refugees, they lived in isolation. For some Hmong families, it was the children who had the most contact with the outside world, through school.

America's relationship with the Hmong can be traced to the 1960s. During the Vietnam War, the U.S. Army needed help in Laos, where the North Vietnamese funneled troops and supplies along the Ho Chi Minh Trail into South Vietnam. The Geneva Accords prevented the United States from sending ground troops into Laos, so the CIA recruited and trained the Hmong, an ethnically distinct group living in the hills, to cut off Communist supply lines, ambush the North Vietnamese, and rescue downed U.S. pilots.

U.S. leaders promised the Hmong refuge if it was needed, a pledge that turned out to be prophetic. About 45,000 members of the Hmong army would eventually fight on behalf of the United States, and nearly half of them would be killed or injured battling the North Vietnamese. And when Laos fell to the Communists in 1975, the Hmong fled to refugee camps in Thailand and waited for their chance to come to the United States. Some were still there at the writing of this book.

The fall of Saigon ended the United States' decades-long attempt to keep communism from overtaking all of Vietnam. Meanwhile, the fall of Vientiane ended Laos's six-century-old monarchy. The monarchy was replaced by the Lao People's Democratic Republic, a democratic-sounding organization that was actually ruthlessly authoritarian and intolerant of political dissent. The government threatened and killed Hmong men and women who had sided with the Americans in fighting the Communists.

By 1975, most opposition leaders had fled the country, mostly into the camps across the border in Thailand. The 1984 film *The Killing Fields* memorably portrayed Communist atrocities that left ditches full of bodies in Cambodia; there are similar, if less known, stories from post–Vietnam War Laos. During a congressional hearing I attended in Washington during the summer of 1997, on whether the United States should grant Laos improved trade status, a congressman asked the Hmong who were sitting in the hearing room to raise a hand if they knew of someone who had been killed by government troops in Laos. Every Hmong in the room responded—some raised both hands and stood up, stretching their arms high in the air to make their point.

Two decades later, the government began encouraging private enterprise, and Laos's economy has grown steadily ever since. Even so, the country remains somewhat primitive economically, with no railroads and a limited infrastructure. According to *Freedom House*, a publication that rates countries' political and civil liberties, Laos is one of the world's poorest and most repressive nations. Its government is one of just a handful of Communist states that still exist in the post–cold war world. The publication's description of Laos includes this chilling passage: "By staging a tightly controlled election in February 2002, the ruling Communist party in Laos signaled that it has few plans to loosen its iron-fisted grip on this impoverished Southeast Asian land." Only about half of its nearly six million citizens can read and write; just 44 percent of its women can. There also remains a mystical quality in the way in which Laotians regard the exiled Lao royal family, a sentiment that lingers in many elderly Hmong living in Minnesota.

Yer Xiong lived in one of the aging clapboard houses that line the streets of Frogtown, a working-class neighborhood of St. Paul. Xiong was a fortyish Hmong refugee who looked ten years older the cold September morning when I visited. The homes along the street were dusted with an early snow. Xiong's seventeen-year-old daughter, Pa Houa Yang, answered my knock in red pajamas and flannel shirt and asked me to wait outside.

She invited me inside after five minutes or so, and I sat on a couch behind four black-haired children who were sitting on the floor, entranced by the Sunday morning cartoons. Yang, a senior at Humboldt High School with plans for college, seemed surprised at my ignorance about polygamy in Minnesota. Then she told me about her father, who had eight children with her mother—whom he had divorced—and another child with his second wife. "He just wanted to marry another wife. And then after he and my mother got divorced, he came back and said he wanted to work it out and live here part of the time. But my mom said no," she said. "I go to his house sometimes to help out, and I get along with his wife. But as far as him coming here to live at times, my mother decided she didn't want that, and I supported her."

Yang said she knew girls in school who were already "married"—committed to a boy or young man, but not married legally—and living with their de facto in-laws. As for her close circle of friends, polygamy was not for them. "My friends at school, we talk about it. We're against it," she told me. Regarding her father, Yang said she had mixed emotions. She loved him, but not some of his ideas about marriage. Of his relationship with her mother, she said, "If he really loved her and respected her, he would not marry another woman and would not want to be away from her."

I wanted to know what her mother thought. Xiong, kneeling on the floor in a floral-patterned dress, her black hair pulled tight behind her head, talked as her daughter translated. She had never had a day of formal schooling in Laos. "Back in Laos, wives were treated very bad and couldn't speak their opinion. But in the United States, I see fewer men marrying more than one woman, although some still take a second wife," she said. Yang broke in to make it clear that her mother need not worry about her. She was going to get a college education, travel, have some life experiences and then think about marriage—to one man. "I've learned from what happened to my parents," Yang said, "and it will help me build a strong family in the future."

Chong invited me into his tiny home on St. Paul's East Side with a nod and a smile, and we sat on his couch as I prepared to take notes about his life as a bigamist. I promised that I wouldn't publish his full name in an AP story about polygamy, explaining that he could face prosecution if Ramsey County learned of his identity. Bea VueBenson, who had arranged the meeting and provided translation, explained this to Chong, but he just smiled and shrugged his shoulders.

Chong was fifty-eight, spoke no English, and had two wives and fifteen children. He and his wives had moved from Laos to the United States fifteen years before, and he moved back and forth between his two families. He wore a white T-shirt with "America" printed across the front, and his living room was an amalgam of American and Asian effects: a U.S. flag and a major league baseball cap here; a map of Laos and pictures of Hmong soldiers there.

Chong had been part of the Hmong resistance that helped the Americans during the Vietnam War, fighting in the hills of Laos. He proudly showed me a black-and-white picture of himself as a young man in army fatigues. The years had rounded out his face.

A picture of General Vang Pao hung on the wall next to Chong's military picture. Vang Pao led the Hmong fighting force during the Vietnam War and had since taken on a kind of mythic following among the refugees living in America. Chong smiled broadly and chopped the air with his hands as he recalled that he and the general were from the same clan. I had no reason to doubt his claims about fighting in the war, and I had developed a lot of respect for the Hmong soldiers who had battled the North Vietnamese on behalf of the United States.

Chong said he had lost a son in the war: "He was taken by the Communists," he said, looking at the floor. I steered the conversation back to his two families, and he went on to explain the reasons polygamy continued to find support in his community. "People don't understand the benefits. If you went to a Hmong funeral, you would see big families, and what you would see is a lot of support. I want to have a big family," he said.

Chong's wife, Mao, quietly folded laundry while Chong and I talked. She said nothing until I asked her about Chong's dual life. Mao, like Yer Xiong, had little formal education and didn't put up a fight when Chong went looking for a second wife. She said she didn't want to cause emotional problems for her children and wanted them to have a father at home—even if he was only around part of the time and seemed more like an uncle than their dad. "Yes, I do feel sad sometimes," she said. "I would have preferred to be the only one, but I let him do it, because he would be like an angry child not getting his way."

She saw Vang's other wife at times, and the two women even helped each other with household chores and taking care of each other's children. "There is no hatred between us, because we share the same man," she said. I had trouble understanding her ho-hum attitude, her resignation, so I asked her what, if anything, she had told her daughters about her experience as a plural wife. "I would tell my daughters that if they get married and their husbands took another wife to let them go, and also not to pursue and marry someone else's husband," she said.

Afterward, VueBenson and I spoke for a moment on the sidewalk outside Chong's house. How long did she think all of this would last? It seemed like an untenable situation—at least for Hmong who were middle-aged or older. "The reality is that we come with patterns and values that are hundreds of years old, and to suddenly stop is not realistic," she said. "That doesn't mean we shouldn't go forward."

Chong Thao

OUT THERE BY OURSELVES

Hmong Refugees Help Their Own

Lee Pao Xiong knew what it felt like to be isolated. Fleeing Laos in the mid-1970s, he and his family ended up in a strange corner of the diaspora: an old farmhouse overlooking the Indiana prairie. Fields upon fields, he remembered thinking. There weren't any Asian faces at the airport in Bloomington when the family landed—just the smiling Mennonites who picked them up and drove them to their new home in the country. The Christian hosts tried to make things as normal as possible, buying Xiong's family bags and bags of rice—and then hiring a Japanese woman to cook it for them. It was safe and quiet deep in the American Midwest, and living there beat hiding from soldiers in the jungles of Laos. But it could be lonely and depressing.

The Mennonites "really went out of their way to help us adjust to America," Xiong recalled in his office that overlooked the Mississippi River in Minneapolis. On the weekends, they piled Xiong's family—all eight of them,

including his five brothers and sisters and his parents—
into a van and drove them to Indiana University for
English classes. Often, on the way home, the family
was treated to a favorite American indulgence. "They
bought us doughnuts on the way back from our English
classes. I mean, that was a big deal. We didn't have anything," Xiong said. "But, man, we were isolated. We
were out there all by ourselves."

Xiong and I met just as Minnesota was preparing for
its single largest refugee influx in years. Thousands of
Hmong who were living in a refugee camp in Thailand
called Wat Tham Krabok were getting ready to come to
the Twin Cities. Most of them had been in the squalid
Buddhist temple compound for years, doing little while
waiting for permission to leave for the West. Now, in
2004, their time had come. The State Department was
granting them asylum as political refugees.

Xiong had made it in Minnesota. He was a housing
planner for the city of Minneapolis, sharply dressed in
a navy suit as he moved between morning meetings.
But in thinking about his family's experience and struggles twenty-five years earlier, he remembered the pain.
He intended to take some of the refugees headed for
Minnesota into his home. For those he couldn't directly
help, Xiong pledged to make sure they were steered in
the right direction and found the particular services
they needed. He knew where to look.

The network of relief organizations that had helped

Xiong's family in Indiana and later in Minnesota—such as Lutheran Social Services and Catholic Charities—had performed admirably. Nobody had been nicer or more accommodating than the Indiana Mennonites. But these groups were now supplemented with agencies that were more familiar with Hmong culture and ways of life. Xiong hoped that would make for an easier transition for the newest refugees. "Our culture is very family-oriented. People are waiting to help," he said. "And now we have [organizations], like Lao Family and other groups, who can provide [English classes] and job training, and they're coming to a city that has dealt with this before. That's the good part."

Some Hmong had lived in Minnesota for nearly three decades. They had their own newspapers and businesses. Their children were going to college. Two Hmong were serving in the state legislature. Some demographic snippets suggested that they were fitting in nicely. By 2004, for instance, Hmong businesses in St. Paul, where most of the refugees from Wat Tham Krabok would come to live, numbered four hundred or more.

Besides that, a larger percentage of Hmong in their twenties and thirties in St. Paul owned homes than any other racial group—including whites. "Ten years ago, they were still emerging from public housing," Mark VanderSchaaf, an economist and demographer for the city of St. Paul, said when I called to ask him whether the city could accommodate the newcomers. They had come a long way. VanderSchaaf credited strong family ties within the Hmong community, along with the willingness of extended families and friends to pool their financial resources, for allowing so many Hmong to buy homes.

When Minnesota's refugees and immigrants talked about fitting in, it usually had to do with setting aside old ways of thinking about clans, tradition, and hierarchy. But those mentalities were deeply ingrained in people who had spent years of their lives surviving in the turmoil and oppression of dysfunctional countries. Nobody grasped that better than the young Hmong professionals who had successfully adapted to life in Minnesota. They knew what to expect when the refugees arrived, and they understood what would be needed to help them make the transition. So, with one foot in the old world and the other in the new, they took on a heavy responsibility.

When it came to covering immigrants, the more I reported, the more questions came to light. My wife, Jeanne, was a good sounding board for story ideas. When I asked her about covering the refugees from Wat Tham Krabok, she peppered me with queries: Who was responsible for helping them? Could people who had lived in a camp for years find decent jobs that would pay a living wage? How about the elderly Hmong who couldn't speak English and weren't likely to learn it? What would they do?

Who could say for sure? Religious congregations, government agencies, and Hmong charities were all preparing to help as much as they could. But they could only do so much. The deeper transition—to a new culture and way of life—would take years. As the refugees prepared to come to Minnesota, nobody, with any certainty, could answer my wife's questions.

Xou Xiong and his extended family were the first refugees from Wat Tham Krabok to arrive in Minnesota. Xiong, his wife, and their seven sons, along with his sister-in-law and her husband, landed at Minneapolis-St. Paul International Airport on June 26, 2004. Their arrival was much different from the one Lee Pao Xiong recalled in Indiana. This time, relatives—Asian faces!—greeted the newcomers. Xou Xiong's sister-in-law, Chong Thao, presented the family with flowers. Her husband, Tong Xee Xiong, carried an American flag in the breast pocket of his shirt. "This is like a dream," Xiong told a reporter for the *Minneapolis Star Tribune*, "but it's a dream coming true." The eleven newcomers were the first of about four thousand Hmong who would eventually leave the Thai camp and move to Minnesota.

Lee Pao Xiong, who was thirty-seven, had lived in the United States since 1976. When I arrived at his office, he immediately showed me a picture of the crowded and primitive refugee camp that he had downloaded from the Internet. It looked grim and hopeless, with children running through filthy water in the streets. "This is not going to be easy," he said of the pending mass migration. He had visited the camp in 1997—an uncle and cousin lived there—and he recalled the open sewage and dirty water, as well as the generation of disillusioned and idle Hmong living there. Some of them had lost hope. "There is nothing for them to do there. People just sit around and wait. If someone has relatives in this country, then they can get money and at least buy food. But that's about it," he said.

The Twin Cities had a growing reputation inside Wat Tham Krabok. Some of the refugees already knew about Minnesota and its cold winters and hot summers. After all, many of their friends, cousins, and siblings had been living there for years. During Xiong's visit years before, one woman told him she was eager to come to Minnesota. "When I told her I was from St. Paul, she followed me around saying, 'Do you know this person and that person?'" he recalled with a laugh.

Others in the camp, to Xiong's frustration, still held out hope that Laos would soon fall from Communist control and that they could all someday go home and resume their lives in the hills. For the older refugees, especially, letting go of that dream would be difficult, especially when they arrived in Minnesota and realized that returning to Southeast Asia was likely out of reach forever. "This is going to be some kind of culture shock," Xiong said, taking off his glasses and rubbing his eyes. "You have no idea." When Xiong returned, he sent letters to U.S. Representative Bruce Vento and other lawmakers, urging them to support a mass migration from the Thai camp to the United States.

In the spring of 2004, St. Paul mayor Randy Kelly and a delegation of about twenty civic leaders, including seven who were Hmong, visited the camp, which was housing fourteen thousand people. Kelly met with United Nations officials and Hmong clan leaders and told them of his interest in helping the refugees settle in St. Paul, a city with strong ties to its immigrant past. Among the delegation's gifts to the people in the camp were more than a dozen solar ovens and, of course, stacks of English-language textbooks.

William Yang recalled the culture shock he felt when he arrived in Minnesota in 1980 and went to live in Lanesboro, a farming hamlet among the bluffs of southeastern Minnesota. He had long since left for the Twin Cities and had become the executive director of the Hmong American Partnership, a fraternal organization that supported relocated Hmong families. He was waiting for relatives to make it past a screening check at Wat Tham Krabok. If they could get to Minnesota, he would take them into his home in St. Paul or help them settle in Rochester, where his mother lived. "We can make sure the children get enrolled in school right away, that they get health screening, that they have a place to live and some household goods," he said. "All the necessary things that need to be done."

Most of the refugees ended up with families in St. Paul. Some of the host families were marking their third decade in Minnesota and knew the ins and outs of schools and the social services system. The family ties proved to be important. Some of the women who arrived were second or third wives and part of combined families with a dozen children or more. They would need a lot of support. According to a report Hennepin County released to the media and public agencies as the refugees were arriving, just a third of the adult population that fled Wat Tham Krabok for Minnesota had a formal education. Only half of the children did.

Even with Hmong families and clans in place, it wasn't clear how the new refugees would fit in. Ilean Her, a Hmong refugee who had become the executive director of the state Council on Asian-Pacific Minnesotans, feared that the refugees would be preyed upon by gangs or otherwise taken advantage of. It was a special concern of hers. A few months earlier, she had appeared at a press conference in St. Paul as the Ramsey County attorney spelled out the activities of a prostitution ring involving Hmong girls, many of them runaways. She had tears in her eyes that day as she talked to reporters.

Now, Her was curious how the new refugees would fare. It was a difficult balance to strike. She was grateful for strong family ties and the wealth of Hmong social services in the Twin Cities, but she wondered whether the transition could perhaps be *too* comfortable. Would the refugees be so shielded from Minnesota life that they would fall under the influence of gangs or other bad elements? How much of the culture would become integrated into their new lives? She feared that a seamless incorporation could lead to isolation. "You need to be a bit overwhelmed and be exposed to what life is like here. That has to be part of the transition, to be a little awe-struck," she said. "I'm afraid that some of them won't get that."

Immigrant and refugee services had come a long way since the cold war. Refugees headed for Minnesota could expect to receive the basics: beds, chairs, dishes, utensils, blankets. They also would receive $400 when they arrived and were eligible for three months of public assistance—twice that if they had no family members to provide support. All of that was useful.

The role of the social agencies in helping refugees assimilate was less clear, however. There were fewer interactions between refugees and the social services workers who could ensure they received the proper health services and enrolled their children in school on time. Many people could fall through the cracks. "It does take a village," Patti Hurd, the Lutheran Social Services resettlement expert, told me. Families, social services agencies, churches, charities, individuals—all would be counted on to do their part. "It takes a community to welcome people into the community," she said.

There were reasons to be hopeful about the eventual assimilation of these newest Minnesota Hmong.

Years before, in the summer of 1997, many Hmong from Minnesota—the refugees who had arrived in the 1970s and '80s—were getting their feet wet with American democracy, holding huge rallies and lobbying their congressmen and congresswomen in Washington. It was remarkable, considering the history of their homeland, which had been ruled by monarchs for six centuries, then by Communists for part of the twentieth. Not much had prepared them to organize and lobby on their own behalf in the nation's capital. Many of them had little formal education. What they knew about political activism had mostly been learned during their short time in the United States. I happened to be in Washington, D.C., then, working as a summer reporter for the *Minneapolis Star Tribune.* The paper wanted some coverage of the Hmong who were visiting the capital, and I got the assignment.

That summer was a watershed. In May, about three thousand Hmong military veterans were finally recognized for their role in the Vietnam War, receiving congressional citations in a ceremony at the Vietnam War

Memorial. A month later, dozens of those veterans, most of whom lived in Minnesota and California, hopped on buses and returned to Washington to lobby on behalf of a bill that would make it easier for Hmong to pass citizenship tests by waiving English language and residency requirements.

The veterans, middle-aged and elderly men, said they deserved the break because of their aid to the United States. Without citizenship, many Hmong feared they would lose medical and disability benefits for legal immigrants that had been eliminated a year before when Congress overhauled the welfare system. "They deserve this because they fought for the U.S. and were recruited by the CIA," said Blong Thao, a St. Paul man whose mother-in-law was the widow of a Hmong veteran. Representative Bruce Vento, a champion of a number of Hmong causes (many Hmong lived in the late Democrat's St. Paul district), summed it up in testimony before a congressional panel. "It's not just a matter of citizenship, it's a matter of honor," he said. The bill passed.

I also watched the Hmong as they urged their representatives to vote against normalizing trade relations with the Lao People's Democratic Republic, which continually ranks with the worst of the world's human rights offenders. Many Hmong would eventually embrace the bill, arguing that an open market with the United States would lead to political liberalization in their homeland. But not that summer. The Hmong who came to the

Capitol were some of the most ardent anti-Communists I had ever met; they were still stinging from their experiences in Laos. Their vehemence showed in the lobbying campaign against normalized trade (which would eventually pass, eight years later). They also successfully lobbied for the restoration of the disability benefits that had been cut by Congress.

It was quite a show of grassroots activism, by a new and inexperienced group, to boot. I hoped to convey that determination to the readers back home. In beginning one article for the *Star Tribune,* I wrote, "Hmong veterans who once felt helpless to influence the U.S. government they served in combat learned a vital civics lesson this summer. Coming to Washington, D.C., in unprecedented numbers from Minnesota, California and other states, they found that speaking out can make a difference."

Omar Jamal

THEM AGAINST US

Somalis Find a Unified Voice

Omar Jamal grew up in the Somali capital of Mogadishu, living through dictatorship in the 1970s and civil
war in the '80s. After leaving for stays in Switzerland,
Germany, and England, he fled Somalia for good in
1991. Kenya was another pit stop in the diaspora, followed by Memphis, Tennessee, where he went to college. Finally, Jamal ended up in Minnesota in 1999. Now
here he was on a frigid winter morning—the thermome-
ter read 10 degrees—working out of a cluttered store-
front on Marshall Avenue in St. Paul. A handwritten
sign hanging crookedly on the door read: Somali Justice
Advocacy Center.

Jamal flipped up the collar of his sport coat and covered his ears with his hands. After growing up in the
desert heat of the Horn of Africa, he was always hit hard
by the Minnesota winter. Finally reaching his office and
ducking inside, Jamal let out his breath. "Aaaahhh," he
said, kicking aside the newspapers and boxes littering

the floor. "At least it's warm in here!" The community center was a bare-bones operation with a fax machine, a few old computers, and an old table and chairs. It had a tiny budget and relied on volunteers. Even for a nonprofit activist such as Jamal, it was a spartan life. A grassroots pacifist organization called Friends for a Non-Violent World shared the space.

The center was a clearinghouse for all issues that concerned Somalis. Refugees called Jamal to complain about the police or to ask about the best place to buy groceries or to see how things were going back in the homeland. In that way, the center existed simply to answer questions and solve minor problems. But just as important, it put a public face on a growing and often misunderstood refugee population. Jamal had a dual job. He wanted Somalis living in Minnesota to push aside clan loyalties, get involved in their communities, and embrace life in a free country. And he hoped to be a conduit between the refugees and the powerful institutions around them: the police, the legislature, the public schools.

Jamal's reputation was growing. In a newspaper profile of him, several Somalis complained about his aggressive posture and penchant for getting his name in the paper. I knew what they meant. I first met Jamal on that cold 2002 morning while reporting on the death of Abu Jeilani, a twenty-eight-year-old Somali man whom police had shot. Walking along Franklin Avenue in south Minneapolis, Jeilani had threatened officers with a

machete and a crowbar and ignored their repeated de-
mands to drop his weapons. The officers tried to shock
him into submission with a stun gun, but after that
failed—possibly because of his thick clothing, an investigation determined—they shot him. It turned out that
Jeilani was mentally ill and spoke little English. He was
presumably either irrational or didn't understand the
officers' commands.

A grand jury eventually cleared the six officers involved in the shooting of any criminal wrongdoing, but
Somalis were outraged. So were many other people, and
Jamal fanned the flames. Dozens of Somalis marched
on the street corner where Jeilani was killed and demanded the firing of Police Chief Robert Olson. One
of their chants was "No justice, no peace. Prosecute the
police." Jamal called a news conference after the shooting and blasted the police, telling reporters that the
Twin Cities had become "a slaughterhouse for the immigrants." My editors assigned me to write about the
shooting and, more broadly, the Somali reaction. I asked
Jamal about his comment when we met at the Somali
center. "I probably shouldn't have used those words.
That was a mistake," he admitted.

Jamal, who was twenty-eight when we met, natty in
a white shirt and brown corduroy blazer, had a crusty
demeanor that belied his round face and droopy eyes.
He could also burst out in sudden, startling laughter,
however, and he always extended a hand to greet me.

While we talked, he looked at me intently, and when I asked him where he had grown up and gone to school—simply for use as biographical information in my article—he fired back, "Is this an interrogation? Are you trying to collect information on me?" The photographer who was with me shot a glance my way, and neither of us could tell whether Jamal was joking. I assured him that I was simply trying to learn a few things about the Somali community for a story, nothing more, and we continued our conversation.

But I didn't hold the outburst against him; there was good reason for his paranoia. The fatal shooting was only the latest in a series of events that seemed to be taking their toll on morale in the Somali community. The previous October, a sixty-six-year-old Somali man died after he was punched and fell to the sidewalk at a Minneapolis bus stop. In November, shortly after the terrorist attacks in New York and Washington, the federal government closed several money-transfer offices in Minneapolis that Somalis were using to send money to relatives, saying the cash was likely being funneled to terrorists.

About two hundred Somalis turned out for a vigil in a show of solidarity and to oppose the closing of the money-transfer offices. Just a month before Jeilani was killed, ten Somalis who had either broken the law or were in the United States illegally were quietly deported. In light of that, Jamal thought Minnesotans would forgive a bit of supercharged rhetoric and accept his overall point that Somalis had reason to be upset. "I really think that Minnesotans should know how the Somali community feels about the circumstances they are in," he said. "I think, after what has happened the last couple of months, it is very understandable, the frustration and anger the community expresses."

Sitting beside Jamal was Jamal Adam, a twenty-four-year-old volunteer at the Somali Justice Advocacy Center and a student adviser at Minneapolis Community and Technical College. He was more philosophical about the struggles within the Somali community and mainly concerned about how American society was organized. He felt a strain between what he considered the affluent and competitive nature of American life and the poor, clan-based society he had known as a child.

"In Somalia, there is more of a collectivist society. People are closer, so the Somali community here is very close," he explained. Also, looking at history, he noted that the Cedar-Riverside Neighborhood in Minneapolis—a refuge for many African immigrants, who lived in low-rent or subsidized housing and opened restaurants and shops there—was once a haven for Swedish immigrants. "That little neighborhood has been part of the whole human movement to this part of the world, a hundred years ago and again today," he said. "I think Minnesotans can understand our fears by looking at their own history and cultural background.

The pace of cultural integration can be slow." Both Jamal and Adam asked me to write that, while they were upset at recent events, Somalis wanted to thank Minnesotans for their welcome.

Somalia, for most Minnesotans, was a little-known nation in the Horn of Africa until 1992, when the United States led an international humanitarian mission into Mogadishu. The intervention ended in urban warfare. Militia fighters killed 18 U.S. soldiers and dragged some of their bodies through the streets, a debacle depicted in the book and movie *Black Hawk Down*. Everyone would soon learn more about Somalis and their civil war, thanks to twenty-four-hour cable television and the United States' acceptance of its refugees.

What they learned wasn't heartening. The country of about eight million people was one of the poorest and most politically oppressed nations in Africa. As *Freedom House* wrote a decade later, "Civil war, starvation, banditry, brutality, and natural disasters ranging from drought to flood to famine have racked Somalia" for nearly two decades. Famine and civil strife caused three hundred thousand deaths in 1991 and 1992. Somalia, which gained independence in 1960, last had a central government in 1991, when the regime of President Mohammed Siad Barre was deposed after warring with militias.

For the most part, the country has existed in a state of perpetual civil war for a dozen years. Clans continued to stake their claim across the land. In the north, for instance, factions declared an independent Republic of Somaliland in 1991. The Puntland is a neighboring region that had governed itself since 1998 but had not claimed independence. In the aftermath of Siad Barre's ouster, power fell along lines of ethnic and clan loyalties, with guerrilla movements and militias vying for supremacy. A transitional government formed in neighboring Djibouti in 2004 held out hope that security could finally be returned to the country.

Somalia was an Islamic state where religious freedom—especially for the few Christians or those of other faiths there—was either absent or only loosely respected. Torture and beatings were common, and journalists, despite official press freedom in the country, faced harassment and had to rely on their clans for protection. The chaotic system that dominated Somalia—a system that decimated the educational establishment and the health care sector—was reflected in its average life expectancy of forty-six years. That was three full decades less than the average life span of an American.

Somalis fleeing that turmoil began arriving on America's shores in the mid-1990s, many of them ending up in Minnesota, Ohio, and other states in the Midwest. State demographers estimate that about 25,000 Somalis now live in Minnesota, though community activists believe there are 50,000 or more.

The Somali Justice Advocacy Center fit a historical pattern. Joel Wurl, the associate director of the Immigration

History Research Center at the University of Minnesota in Minneapolis, noted that it started out as a place for Somalis to call if they needed help with the basics, such as where to take English classes. But over time, after clashes with the establishment, it became an outlet for protest and political expression. "It's fairly typical for immigrant groups to generate these kinds of self-help groups first—what we used to call fraternal organizations—and then branch out to larger concerns: social assistance, cultural awareness, and in some cases political activism," Wurl said. Jamal's group had ventured into the rough-and-tumble world of activism.

Some of Minnesota's more recent newcomers had already become part of the establishment. The Minneapolis Police Department, for instance, had about two dozen Asian American officers helping to patrol the city, and St. Paul had elected the first Hmong state legislator in the country. Minneapolis police had a liaison to the Somali community, though he was not on hand when officers were confronting Jeilani. It was all part of a historical pattern, for better or worse. "Africans have come as refugees in the 1990s, at the end of the cold war, and we are still trying to figure out how all this works together," Dianna Shandy, an assistant professor of anthropology at Macalester College in St. Paul, told me.

The meetings between Somali leaders and Minneapolis police bore some fruit. Olson met face-to-face with Jamal, and both men came away pledging their mutual cooperation and vowing to keep the lines of communication open. Mayor R. T. Rybak ordered public agencies to review how they responded to crises involving the mentally ill. Immediately, he demanded that security guards in the public housing authority receive training about Somali and Muslim culture. Such training was also planned for the police force and other city agencies. He thanked Somalis for their help. Olson continued as police chief.

Mahamoud Wardere taught English to Somali students at Pillsbury Elementary. But teaching at the Minneapolis school wasn't his only interest. A natural leader, he wasted little time after moving to Minnesota, running for mayor in 2001 (finishing eleventh out of twenty-two candidates in a Democratic-Farmer-Labor Party primary). Undaunted by the electoral loss, he spent much of his time broadening his political awareness and media savvy through the League of Women Voters and other groups.

Wardere invited me to his apartment one afternoon a few weeks after the police shooting. It was calm and cool in the dimly lit room, with red drapes covering the windows. One of his children crawled around on his lap and occasionally over to mine to play with my tape recorder. Wardere had a bright smile and the habit of starting a sentence softly and quietly, then building to a loud and animated delivery as he became more excited.

"The shooting, yes, it created fear, but I don't know of a single Somali who is moving away," he said. "It was scary to our community. Two children I teach were [shooting victim Jeilani's] relatives, and a lot of people had the opinion that they should not have shot him. I think it has nothing to do with hate, but it's more of a failure of our mental health system." Then, waving his hands in a crossing fashion as if to change the subject, Wardere continued, "First of all, I should say that the United States is the best place to live, no matter what has happened. Our acceptance here and the respect we've been shown, that has been very good." That was the kind of opening line I had gotten used to. Many immigrants took pains to point out how much they liked Minnesota before dropping the hammer and laying out the ways in which they'd been mistreated. The basic message was: "We like it here a lot, but . . ."

In this case, the "but" was a basic feeling of second-class status among Somalis, manifested in Jeilani's shooting, the deportations, and the general paranoia and suspicion among Muslims after the September 11, 2001, terrorist attacks. Many immigrants, after they had lived here for a while, felt that America's most marketable ideas—respect for free speech and religion, economic opportunity, a fondness for individual achievement, its celebration of cultures—seemed somehow watered down. And there were small-fry issues, such as confusion over social niceties, which also created problems. "Language and cultural situations are a big thing," Wardere said. "In Somalia, we don't have to say 'thank you' all the time. But here in Minnesota, people are always saying 'thank you' for everything! Now, we are not being rude, we are just not used to that custom. So you can see that it can be tough making adjustments."

Wardere couldn't wait for another chance to run for office. (He had a sense of humor about his chances of getting elected. "After 9/11, I know that when people see a name like mine on the ballot, they think twice!" he said with a laugh.) The deportations struck immigrants as particularly cruel since anyone sent back to Somalia was being thrown into a pitiful world of chaos and lawlessness. Many also believed that the offenses for which people were being kicked out of the country were minor—mostly shoplifting and traffic violations, I was told—although immigration officials said the offenses included sex and drug crimes and assault. "We want law and order—that is why we are here!" Wardere said. "We are not advocating that every person be here, but we were shocked by [the deportations]. I should not think that they should be sent back for the things they have done."

It appeared that the Somalis would get a break from the deportations. Over the next several months, federal judges ruled in favor of Somalis who had been threatened with being made to leave the country. Judge John Tunheim of U.S. District Court in Minneapolis, in a case involving Keyse Jama, a Somali man who lost his legal residency status after pleading guilty to an assault, ruled that it was illegal for the federal government to deport anyone to Somalia, since that country had no functioning government that could accept them. A U.S. District Court judge in Seattle followed suit, issuing a nationwide ban on deportations of Somalis until the courts resolved whether it was legal.

In January of 2005, however, the U.S. Supreme Court, in a 5-4 ruling, said the United States can deport immigrants without first getting permission from the receiving country. More than eight thousand Somalis being held around the country for possible deportation, many of them in Minnesota jails, awaited hearings that would determine their fate. Jama was flown to Somalia—then returned when the government there wouldn't accept him.

It wasn't easy to predict who would fit in in Minnesota. I met several refugees, for instance, who had gone to school in Europe or in the United States but still felt like outcasts in Minnesota. They held good jobs and handled the English language well. But cultural barriers lingered, and misunderstandings often felt like slights. When a Somali woman went missing in Minneapolis in the spring of 2006, three Somalis called me to complain that rescue and recovery crews weren't trying very hard to find her.

Call it the Minnesota Nice in me, but I didn't believe

those Hennepin County crews were indifferent about the fate of that woman, whose body was later found. When I inquired about it, officials explained that they were doing everything they could, and I believed them. But I also understood where the Somalis were coming from. Back home, they couldn't count on the authorities to do the right thing in such situations. There was no trust. So expecting them to completely trust the powerful institutions around them discounted their history.

Somalis were becoming organized, but it could be slow going. Civil war and political corruption in their homeland had left them wary of authoritarian government and hungering for the democratic kind. At the same time, living in such a tribalized society had done little to create any sense of citizenship or political participation among the Somalis who were now residing in Minnesota.

Jamal Adam, the young man who sat in on my interview with Omar Jamal, said the Somali experience in Minnesota needed to be considered with that troubled history in mind. "We are coming from a place where the government is sort of like them against us. It's the people versus the government," he said. "So when anything happens like the shooting, that triggers past experience, and that affects the whole way people look at government. It reminds them of past fears and experiences."

Ali Galaydh

A MOST URGENT MATTER

Somali Politics, Here and Abroad

Ali Galaydh held forth in the corner of a St. Paul union hall. He had to talk loud to be heard over the Bruce Springsteen song filling up the room, but the Somalis surrounding him leaned in to hear. They had reason enough to listen: A few years before, Galaydh had led an interim Somali government formed with high hopes of repairing the breach caused by the civil war there. The temporary government never actually took power, and Ali Galaydh the professor never became Ali Galaydh the prime minister. He ended up in Minnesota, instead. But he had a following.

The men had come to a rally for John Edwards, the Democratic vice presidential candidate. For the first time, some Somalis had organized a political group in Minnesota, and they were backing the Kerry-Edwards ticket. Galaydh himself—no stranger to political combat—was readying to take part in his local caucus, evaluating candidates and platforms.

Somalis, in a change from the 2000 campaign, were volunteering for candidates and helping refugees who had obtained citizenship to vote. They were mobilizing, and fast. "I think, especially in the last two years or so, a good number of Somalis here have become naturalized and become organized," Galaydh said.

Galaydh wore a suit and tie, like many of the Somalis at the rally. They were much better dressed than the rest of the Minnesotans who stood among them in khakis and flannel shirts. I had the feeling they wanted to stand out—that they had put on their best clothes in honor of political participation itself. For many of them, it was the first legitimate political rally they had ever attended, with a choice in national leadership before them. It was a cherished moment.

The election season inspired Somalis to try something new. Taking stock of the divisions among them, they envisioned their own elected council that would represent Somalis wherever they lived in Minnesota. They were scattered, with enclaves in the Twin Cities and Rochester, and in small towns like Willmar, Marshall, and Owatonna. The council wouldn't have any real power, but it would be a way for them to avoid the ugly clan rivalries and prejudices that lingered from the old country.

Mohamoud Mohamed was trying to sell the idea. He ran a social services agency for immigrants and refugees who lived in central Minnesota. For the time being, the St. Cloud Area Somali Salvation Organization was operating out of Mohamed's apartment. He had moved the agency out of a south side office, partly because of financial shortfalls but also because someone had spray-painted it with racist graffiti and set it on fire. The agency had once doubled as a grocery store and community center for Somalis and other African immigrants, and it was also the first mosque in St. Cloud. But on the day we met, it was just a promising fraternal group without a permanent home. So Mohamed and I met at a coffee shop.

The council seemed like an odd concept to me. I didn't know of any other ethnic groups—at least among the new immigrants and refugees I was meeting—that had created their own elected bodies. I figured some Somalis would think of the council as their own mini-legislature. Besides that, I wondered, who would administer the elections? Where would they be held? It seemed a little pie-in-the-sky and potentially divisive.

Mohamed said I was wrong about all of that. He said such a body would be a modernizing force by encouraging Somalis to set aside clan loyalties and disagreements about the civil war back home. It could help them find common ground.

"Most of the refugees here lost relatives in the civil war—a war that is still ongoing. So there is bitterness," he said. Mohamed had met with clan leaders to discuss the council, and he told them, "Whether you belong to this tribe or that tribe, this is the reality. Let's work on it." He pushed them to have a knock-down, drag-out debate and air their differences. "It will be up to the council to make people understand how to use their influence in a civilized way—the right way," he said. "We need to solve peacefully what we couldn't solve by the gun in Somalia."

Abdulkadir Mohamed joined us for coffee. The Somali elder (no relation to Mohamoud Mohamed), a brown cardigan draped over his bony shoulders, nodded in agreement as the younger Mohamed spoke. He clasped his hands together in a tight fist, telling me that the council was about unity. They needed that more than anything, he said. Mohamoud Mohamed said leaders hoped to organize slates of candidates who would compete for the council that summer. From Minneapolis to Faribault to Willmar, wherever there were Somalis, they would come out to vote.

Getting the elections organized across a state as vast as Minnesota proved difficult, however. The elections were delayed—until the fall and then beyond.

Somalis weren't only interested in their state of affairs in Minnesota. For older refugees, especially, the politics of their homeland often took center stage. It was the ultimate question for the older generation who, the longer they lived in Minnesota, felt their identity being swept away by American culture. If they were ever to return home, to go back to their roots, they would need to do it soon.

An interim government formed in Djibouti in 2004 held out the most promising chance yet that Somalia could be delivered from years of chaos and civil war. That meant many Somalis who had been out front in speaking up for Somalis living in Minnesota found themselves back in the political arena—only this time on behalf of their homeland. It was a chance they couldn't afford to lose.

In Minnesota, in what had become a center of the Somali diaspora, Somalis furiously debated the proper course of action in securing a peaceful homeland. The transitional government had formed during peace talks and was divided after the president set up operation in Jowhar, a city about sixty miles northwest of Mogadishu, the Somali capital.

The Minnesota Somalis argued over two main issues: whether Somalia should allow Ethiopian and Kenyan troops into the country to help provide security, and whether the United Nations should lift an arms embargo on Somalia. Somalis on both sides of that argument went to work on perhaps their best hope for getting the issue addressed in the United States Congress: the Minnesota senatorial delegation of Norm Coleman, a Republican, and Democrat Mark Dayton.

I went to the Cedar-Riverside neighborhood to meet Galaydh, a lecturer at the University of Minnesota. He arrived in a charcoal gray suit and deep red tie that off-set his sparse beard and graying hair. Galaydh brought his experience as a politician and expatriate to his discussions of international relations and government at the Hubert H. Humphrey Institute of Public Affairs.

At Mapps Coffee & Tea, we sat under a crooked map of Africa. Galaydh dropped a sheaf of papers in front of me, including letters that had been delivered to Coleman and Dayton. He and several other Somalis had recently visited the senators in their Washington offices to talk about the interim government and to urge them to oppose help from Kenya and Ethiopia—known as "frontline" states—as well as the lifting of the arms embargo. It had been a whirlwind tour, and Galaydh was especially excited about having the ear of Coleman, who had a position on the influential Senate Foreign Relations Committee.

"It has moved the debate," he asserted about the results of his group's lobbying effort. "Coleman told me, 'We want to keep our eye on the ball.'" Coleman had said publicly that he was seeking support from other members of Congress "to help bring greater U.S. support for a stable and democratic government in Somalia." Galaydh gave me a crash course in Somali politics and argued against the presidency of Abdullahi Yusuf, whom he regarded as corrupt and out of touch. He feared there would be continued violence in Somalia as long as militias held sway throughout the country. "I feel we need to disarm the militia and make sure any arms coming into the country will find their way into the hands of the government—not the militias. I'm extremely worried about violence breaking out."

Galaydh sensed a historic chance for his homeland and was doing what he could from his post thousands of miles away in the American Midwest. He was grateful for the refuge he found in Minnesota and for the opportunity to teach. But he revered his home country and his upbringing there. "I come from a generation of Somalis who benefited from living there. From third grade through getting a Ph.D., I received public help, so I feel obligated to contribute at this critical time," he said.

Across the river in St. Paul, where another coffeehouse served as a Somali salon, I met with Omar Jamal. Jamal had just returned from a trip to New York, where Yusuf had given a speech before several hundred Minnesotans, including twenty Somali women from Minneapolis who had flown with Jamal to New York. He appeared tired and leaned against a booth, one foot on a chair in front of him. "How are you?" he said. "I should ask how *you* are—you look worn out," I answered.

Jamal was also committed to a stable Somalia, yet, unlike Galaydh, he supported the interim government's call for military help from bordering states as well as the lifting of the UN arms embargo. "I'm not looking for a perfect government here. It's a country that has gone through fifteen years of civil war. They need to have law and order as soon as possible. In order to have any government succeed, you have to have security."

Jamal's group had also been giving Coleman the full-court press. About a month earlier, at a discussion at Hamline University that involved the British ambassador to the United States, Somalis cheered the senator. Jamal was increasingly convinced that the Republican was seeing things his way. "We are thankful for him," he said.

Coleman had indeed met with a spokesman for Abdullahi Yusuf and had talked to Yusuf himself on the phone. His spokesman said Coleman wanted Congress to focus its attention on the tiny African country. A few weeks later, Coleman announced plans to introduce a resolution in the Senate committing the United States to helping the Somali interim government. Dayton, too, had met with two former Somali lawmakers and the current Somali speaker. The lobbying effort, measured by the incremental steps of refugees, was paying off.

Other newcomers in Minnesota were clinging to life in their homelands. Cell phones, Web newspapers, and the flowering of blogs were offering easy communication and an endless stream of information.

Samuel Kofi Woods was a human rights activist who fled Liberia in the late 1990s when the dictator Robert Taylor ran the country. Threatened by the regime, Woods first came to Minnesota because an uncle lived here; he stayed and made the state his home base for a continued campaign of promoting human rights in Liberia and its neighboring countries. He remained in close contact with other dissidents and Liberians in the diaspora, and his work also took him to Washington and New York and back to Africa.

By the time Woods was fleeing for America, as many as 150,000 people in Liberia were dead as the result of civil strife. They had been killed in a decade of fighting that began when Taylor launched a guerrilla war against a military regime that itself had taken power in a coup. The country's history was chaotic.

Liberia finally had a successful and legitimate democratic election in 2005, and Woods braced himself for the exhilarating prospect of returning home. His years of work were paying off. Newly elected president Ellen Johnson-Sirleaf had appointed him as the country's labor minister. But Woods wasn't so sure he would return to Liberia right away or whether his children, two of them American college students, would even join him there. He, too, had grown to like Minnesota and especially the Twin Cities. He was split between two worlds.

"I haven't been as focused on things happening in the U.S. or in Minnesota as I have on the [Liberian] border states," he said in January 2006. "But with this election in Liberia, lots of refugees are interested in returning, in dignity and in the process where human rights are not violated by the government. So I have to be involved with that right now."

Even the tiny ethnic Karen rebel group of Myanmar had a dissident leader living in Minnesota.

Mahn Robert BaZan, the son of a former Karen National Union president, moved to Minnesota in 2000 after three decades as a guerrilla fighter in Myanmar, the country once better known as Burma. BaZan would talk to anyone about the Karens' plight, and he immediately invited me for a visit when I called. He was animated and happy, with a smile that quickly broke into a frown when the subject turned to the grave dangers of being Karen.

BaZan was up against one of the most ruthless regimes in the world. The Myanmar military took power in 1962, ruling by decree, choking the press, and suppressing basic human rights through such chilling tactics as jailing democracy activists. The Karen National Union was one of a handful of rebel groups that continued to antagonize the government, playing off of the United States' refusal to deal with the country.

Yet BaZan kept the faith. Out of his brick apartment building in St. Paul, he organized rallies and maintained contact with Karen exiles living in the diaspora. A rally at the state capitol in the summer of 2005 drew a few hundred supporters—a decent start to what he hoped would be a growing consciousness of the Karen movement in the West.

It wasn't difficult—with cell phones, e-mail, and the Internet—to stay connected to the independence movement and have some influence while living thousands of miles away. Minnesotans were interested in BaZan's cause—and even supportive once they learned about Myanmar's totalitarian regime and its treatment of Aung San Suu Kyi, a human rights activist and Nobel Peace Prize laureate who for years lived under house arrest. So BaZan felt at home. He had only one complaint about Minnesotans and their famed provincialism. "They need to know that we are not Korean," he said with a laugh. "We are Karen. *Karen!*"

Such dual allegiances could linger for years—even decades. In the St. Paul suburb of North Oaks, Croatian refugee Boris Mikšić, who had fled Yugoslavia in the 1970s during Tito's reign, ran a successful business enterprise while also holding a seat on the Zagreb city council. He kept close tabs on Zagreb life, fielded constituent concerns on his Web site, and visited the city once a month. Mikšić had no plans to leave Minnesota. But his roots in the state ran much deeper than they did for Minnesota's newest immigrants, and he saw the inherent conflicts for refugees who lived here and fought for causes abroad.

The problem was that refugees often lost touch with

local concerns in their zeal for change back home—a recipe for alienation. "Immigrants come to the U.S. and bring their conflicts and problems with them, and that's not great, and it's not the American way," Mikšić said. "But I found that Minnesota people are very supportive, and they're curious. They're interested in what's happening in the world."

For these refugees, it felt right living in Minnesota while working on problems in their homelands.

Abbas Mehdi was a professor at St. Cloud State University and founder of an exile dissident group devoted to democracy in Iraq. In 2005, two years after the American invasion to oust Saddam Hussein, he went home for the first time in three decades. He hoped someday to return for good.

Refugee life was different than it used to be in the American Midwest or other places far from the centers of power, he said. It was still sort of a no-man's-land for some people, especially those who yearned for home. But it was a no-man's-land with cell phones and the Internet, the communication tools that made all the difference. "If it weren't for technology, I probably wouldn't be living in Minnesota," he said. "The world has changed."

Whenever I talked with refugees about their troubled homelands, they could barely hold back their anger. It hardly mattered where they had come from; they were refugees for a reason, after all, and it was never a pleasant one. Back home, the leadership was corrupt, or no one was safe, or there was famine and war. Yet many new-comers still wanted to return someday and even planned on it as if it were only a matter of time. The Karen, for instance, dreamed about a return to Myanmar—just as soon as the military regime could be overthrown by a few guerrilla fighters. Even many Somalis, who came from one of the most hopeless places on the planet, vowed one day to go home.

I never really understood all of that optimism in the face of so much despair. Did they really think they would ever go back? There was no government in Somalia, a one-party regime in Laos, a fragile democracy in Liberia. The list was long. It would be many years, I thought to myself, before anyone would be going anywhere.

It was easy to get a little cynical. But in covering Min-nesota's refugees, you had to be open to possibilities. To me, in some odd way, those hopes and dreams were part of the refugees' appeal. After all of that turmoil back home—maybe because of it—they remained deeply connected to their roots and determined to see life re-turn to normal there. How could you not pull for them?

For many Somalis living in Minnesota, as one Somali elder put it, the fate of the interim government "was of the most urgent matter." The future of Somalis reach-ing middle age and beyond—their chance to ever return home—was tied to the fate of the temporary government.

Another failed government could mean that many Somalis would never leave Minnesota. Many Somalis had been living in the United States for more than a decade and sensed the connections to their homeland slipping away.

Meanwhile, many younger Somalis, while united in their hope for a peaceful homeland, were ambivalent about what the new government could mean for them. Some considered themselves to be Minnesotans, or Americans, more than Somali. These younger Somalis, like so many immigrants and refugees, were being pulled in different directions. Where did their ultimate sympathies—and their hopes and dreams—lie? Here in Minnesota, where they had grown up and been educated? Or back in their homeland, the land of their forefathers, traditions, and ways of life?

I met with five Somali men, ages twenty-seven to thirty-three, all of them college students or recent graduates, in downtown Minneapolis to ask them what the prospects of a stable Somalia meant for them. Toting backpacks and cups of coffee, the men gathered around me at a small table. We shook hands and I explained that I wanted to write a story about the influence Somalis living in Minnesota were having on the politics of Somalia.

"We are very passionate about this topic," said Jamal Adam, the young man who had spoken to me a few years earlier, after Minneapolis police shot and killed a mentally disabled Somali. "It is second on the list of issues we are passionate about," he added, smiling broadly, "behind women!" Everyone laughed, but Jamal began waving his hands and shaking his head. "Don't print that!" he pleaded. "Don't print that!" Adam was the de facto moderator of a political bullshit session. Most of the men followed Somali news on newspaper Web sites and blogs, though Adam was taking a break from all of it because he feared it was causing disunity more than anything. "I needed to take some time off," he said, exhaling and settling back into his chair.

Mukhtar Gaaddasaar, a recent University of Minnesota graduate, said many Somalis his age had been in the United States since grade school and had fewer connections to Somalia than their parents. They liked Minnesota. "Many Somalis living in the diaspora are out of touch. As for myself, I think with the education I have I could make it [in Somalia], but I'm not sure I would live there forever even if I decided to go back."

All of them seemed to be ambiguous about the future of Somalia and whether they would ever find it stable enough to return—or whether the nation would ever offer the opportunities they were finding in Minnesota. The likelihood seemed small, at least in the near future. Even so, they wanted the new government to work. When I asked Adam about the possibility that the government could once again fail—dooming the country and its people to more years of disorder—he shook his head and pursed his lips, looking grim. "That," he answered, "is the unthinkable."

The men realized they had the unique opportunity to study and work in Minnesota while safely detached from the turmoil that burdened Somalia and much of Africa. They revered the strong family ties and traditions of their heritage. But they also embraced ambition and individualism, and they held clan distinctions at bay. They wanted to be engineers, college professors, and business leaders—things they could only hope to be in their native land; things most people in America took for granted.

"I would like to take back to Somalia the civic culture that we have here so they can move forward from clan kinship to something that is greater," Jamal said as I got up to leave, gathering my notebook and pen into my bag. "This is the greatest asset that we can bring to the country."

Ahmed Wassie

LIVING IN DENIAL

Ethiopians Take on HIV/AIDS

Redwan Hamza, reclining deep in his chair and clasping his hands behind his head, brushed aside my complaints about the July heat wave. Wearing a black T-shirt and a big smile, he seemed in defiance of the sweltering temperature. "We make do," he said with a laugh. "Nope. No A.C. in here!" A squeaky fan blew some stale air around as I tugged at my collar and felt the sweat trickling down my arms. Hamza ran a center called Oromo Community of Minnesota in the Cedar-Riverside neighborhood of Minneapolis, near the West Bank of the University of Minnesota campus. The fans and used furniture were further reminders of the shoestring budgets that held many immigrant community centers together.

Cedar-Riverside had an international flavor that seemed to fit Hamza and his Afro-centric organization. I was early for our meeting, so I took a stroll along the street, checking out some of the ethnic cafés and shops.

There was an African grocery and coffee shop, a Mexican restaurant, and a Muslim meat market, to name just a few businesses that traded in ethnic fare. Old men who had probably lived most of their lives in Africa—and seemed starkly out of place in Minneapolis—visited on street corners. Women in scarves or body-covering burkas moved in and out of the stores.

Hamza was an ambassador for the neighborhood and the African refugee community. He was part proselytizer for Oromo (40 percent of Ethiopians are ethnic Oromos) and part community activist, promoting independence for Oromo one minute and doling out advice about local schools and hospitals the next. The community center offered training in "Oromo Culture, history, language, etc.," according to its stated mission. But like the Somali center across the river in St. Paul, it was more of a catchall for African immigrant concerns. Workers at the center taught English, tutored immigrant children, and counseled elders who were struggling to adjust to American life. For Africans of all stripes who needed a place to gather and talk things over, Hamza's center was the place to go.

It was also a crucial center in an important health struggle. In 2002, the state Health Department discovered a sobering trend: HIV and AIDS cases among African immigrants and refugees living in Minnesota were on the rise. Health workers had identified forty-six new HIV or AIDS cases among African immigrants in 2001— nearly twice the number of new HIV or AIDS cases reported among that group the year before. Many of the cases involved people who had contracted HIV in Africa and brought it with them, and their presence in Minnesota—especially if the virus continued to spread—promised to become a major health concern. As a longtime Ethiopian refugee, Hamza played an important role in educating and helping Ethiopians who were new to American culture. Now, the Health Department was asking for his help in fighting one of the great scourges of the times.

Cultural taboos would make it difficult to counter the trend. Ethiopians, reserved and conservative in many ways, rarely talked about AIDS or other sexually transmitted diseases. That made for a sensitive task: forcing the religious and social mores of Ethiopians and other Africans through the cultural strainer. Hamza was working hard to promote the educational workshops that he ran out of his youth center, but it wasn't easy. As he told me with a resigned laugh, "There is such a stigma about AIDS that if we simply announce, 'Hey, come for AIDS education,' no one would show up! It's just not talked about. You don't talk about sex in public!"

One problem, Hamza reported, was getting the proper written materials that could be handed out in the community and actually read. As far as he knew, there wasn't anything that he considered "culturally or linguistically" appropriate. He hoped to bring together physicians, Health Department workers, and translators to create some brochures. "If we can reach the population, we can make a difference," he said. But he sounded less than hopeful when he elaborated on what was sure to be a tough battle ahead.

"What we have to worry about is that the issue of AIDS is a stigma in most African communities. People don't want to talk about it. People don't want to know about it," he said. "For those who are infected with the disease, they will think that that person is terrible and all of those things attached to them." There were some progressive Christians in the African community—a result of decades of missionary work in Africa—but that was about it. As for the topic of homosexuality among his circle of friends, Hamza said, "From my experience, I've never heard anybody talk about that type of thing."

Health Department statistics showed a steady rise in HIV infections among African refugees in Minnesota in the 1990s. Seven cases were reported in 1990; forty-six were reported eleven years later. In 2001, 16 percent of the new HIV cases in Minnesota were in the African immigrant community, which made up less than 1 percent of the state's population of about 4.9 million people. Those forty-six cases represented a 39 percent jump from the number reported two years earlier.

Tracy Sides, a state epidemiologist who worked on the HIV/AIDS issue, hoped a grassroots educational campaign could be launched in the Twin Cities. But she knew it would be a difficult task. After speaking with other health workers and community leaders such as Hamza, she thought the best way to raise awareness would be through ethnic newspapers, community forums, radio shows—even plays or brief dramatic performances that touched on HIV/AIDS.

Radio seemed to offer the surest way to reach a broad audience in the immigrant community. By the early 2000s, the small, independent Twin Cities station KFAI had a program for just about every ethnic group in the Twin Cities, including *Khmers in Minnesota, Somali Voices, Hmong Wameng, Filipino American National News, Radio Ukraine, Vietnam Minnesota Radio,* and *Eritrean Community Radio.* Sides herself sat in on some of the broadcasts, offering Health Department perspectives on important issues and feeling at times like her task was quixotic. "There's a wide spectrum on how comfortable people are talking about this," she said of the HIV/AIDS figures. "Sure, there has been some distribution of condoms and things like that, but it's just not as effective as it should be right now. The traditional American person has been exposed to this for years, but you can't make that assumption for African immigrants."

Besides referring me to Hamza, Sides suggested that I speak with Ribka Berhanu, an Ethiopian woman who worked as a women's health advocate in the Health Department. Berhanu was also involved with the Minnesota

AIDS Project, a nonprofit organization whose efforts focused on raising awareness about HIV/AIDS and helping those who were living with the disease. She told me she had emigrated five years earlier, and I asked her about the AIDS crisis in Ethiopia. Her response was stark: "Every time I call home, I hear of a new person who has HIV, or that someone has committed suicide because they have it. That's the culture [African immigrants] are coming from."

Despite all her work on HIV/AIDS awareness, Berhanu wasn't hopeful about making much progress, at least in the short term. Too many people were becoming infected because they either ignored warnings about safe sex or held fast to myths about how the disease was contracted. She echoed Hamza's concern about the lack of effective written material for the immigrant community. "I can't say we are doing well because of a total shortage of information that is appropriate for people coming from other countries. You would need things in a huge number of languages—there are so many differences among the different groups, there really isn't anything out there. I can't think of one single pamphlet," she said.

I asked Berhanu to explain the stigma that prevented candid conversations about AIDS. That even an educated community leader like Hamza found discussions about HIV/AIDS a rarity in his circle of friends surprised me. "People don't want other people to know they've been out there having sex. There is that fear. But it's a deeper issue than that," she explained. "There's just a lack of knowledge. Certain clients come here and tell us their families won't let them eat and play with children who have HIV because they're afraid they might get it."

Most of Minnesota's African immigrants and refugees were concentrated in the Twin Cities, with a handful in smaller towns such as St. Cloud, Rochester, and Willmar. By 2000, the census showed that as many as thirty-five thousand African-born people were living in Minnesota, many of them refugees from civil strife in Somalia and Ethiopia. No one could put a finger on the exact number of Africans in the state, but it was clear that HIV and AIDS were hitting them disproportionately hard.

The Health Department said that at the end of 2001, 266 Africans living in Minnesota had HIV or AIDS. Most of them, health officials believed, were already infected at the time they arrived in the United States. That wasn't surprising, since in Ethiopia alone, about three million people had AIDS—roughly 10 percent of the sexually active population. The country had just two known cases in 1986. By contrast, about 4,300 people in Minnesota—less than one-tenth of 1 percent of the population—were infected with HIV/AIDS in 2001.

Compared with other urban centers around the

country, the numbers in Minnesota were low. That was a good thing all around. But the relatively small number of cases in Minnesota fueled the fantastic assumption among some African immigrants, so I was told, that no one had AIDS in America. Combined with myths about how the disease is transmitted, that illusion led to a behavioral complacency among some of those people who were most at risk. That is what most concerned health officials.

Writing about HIV/AIDS was tricky. Like polygamy, trying to explain what was happening without giving Ethiopians and other African refugees a bad name posed some risky terrain. Yet here, too, the cultural strainer sifted harmful traditions of silence on sexual matters while protecting the admirable, close-knit family ties of African immigrants. It was a prime example of the difficulty of assimilation. You couldn't completely understand the African immigrant experience without taking a close look at this crisis.

When I look back at a decade of reporting on these issues, I don't recall the details of the stories I wrote as much as I remember my encounters with people. In the case of HIV/AIDS—a difficult subject for everyone involved—the response showed how cooperation often rose to the surface when it was needed.

The state often called on immigrants and refugees for help. Language interpretation was the most obvious and immediate need in Minnesota, especially in matters of public health and safety. Nothing was more urgent than curbing HIV and AIDS cases.

But workers or liaisons were also needed to explain the how and the why of the large institutions that many newcomers found confusing and frightening. The tax system, for instance, was a civic concept that many immigrants—especially refugees from broken and corrupt countries—little understood. Like combating HIV/AIDS, it would take an educational campaign and the help of refugees themselves to make it work.

In the early 2000s, the state Department of Revenue hired people from four emerging groups of newcomers—the Hmong, Vietnamese, Somalis, and Hispanics—for the specific task of fostering assimilation. Their job was to help coordinate an outreach program that would teach immigrants and refugees about the tax system and how to file their annual returns. The government had a vested interest in getting its money, for sure. But in reality, most immigrants' wages were low enough that they qualified for state and federal tax credits—refunds that amounted to hundreds if not thousands of dollars. The bigger issue was getting new Minnesotans into the habit of preparing for and taking part in the great American obligation of paying Uncle Sam. They needed to know why they paid taxes, where the money went, and how to do it. That required a level of trust.

It was no easy task. Gloria Gazdik, who ran the

outreach program, said that to many immigrants, taxation was nothing more than "institutional robbery." It didn't help that in 2004 the state accused eleven Somali tax preparers of attempting to inflate their clients' refunds. Officials caught about 3,500 questionable returns—filed primarily on behalf of Somalis—and stopped payment on about $3 million in unwarranted refunds. But the damage was done. African immigrants didn't know how to pay their taxes, many didn't trust the government, and tax preparers from their own communities were preying on them. A better system was clearly needed.

One of the state's immigrant hires was Sadik Farah. Farah was working on his MBA at the University of St. Thomas and had the perfect combination of traits for the job: He was organized, good with numbers, and proud of his East African heritage. Nearly every newcomer who called his office with questions about taxes could expect to get an answer. "If somebody calls us and speaks another language, we will find someone to talk to them, no problem," he said.

Minnesota had established more than three hundred sites around the state where low-income workers could get their taxes prepared for free. Most new immigrants and refugees qualified, and the state had interpreters for about ten languages at the sites. At an alternative high school in the Cedar-Riverside neighborhood of Minneapolis, where workers had set up makeshift booths in an empty warehouse, volunteers spoke English, Somali, Amharic, and Hmong. When they weren't helping customers, they handed out juice and cookies.

"This is part of a bigger community education program," Farah said. "We are trying to build trust between the immigrant community and the Minnesota Revenue Department. A lot of [immigrants] were mistreated in their home countries, and they carry that here. They have to trust me and see me as part of the community and not somebody who was 'sent' by the government."

Farah, who wore a goatee and hair cropped tightly on the sides, came to the United States in 1997 and seemed to relish his role as a bridge between immigrants and his agency. He looked Western in his gray sweater vest and khakis but easily broke into his native tongue. He was comfortable with the casual bonhomie of East Africans. "It's not only the refugees that need to understand another culture, it's also the Revenue Department, too," he said.

Farah Adan was among the dozens of immigrants who streamed in and out of the warehouse, sitting for ten- or fifteen-minute seminars with CPAs or attorneys fresh from their jobs around town. Adan, who was twenty, was trying to earn his high school diploma while working part-time at the Twin Cities airport, where he drove elderly and disabled passengers around in electric carts. He was eligible for state and tax credits—money he would need badly as he struggled to get through school and pay the rent—but he thought he owed the government some money. "I wondered, 'Why are they going to take my money? This is unfair,'" he said. "Since then, I have learned about it, and I now understand that it is OK. But not at first." Adan was told that night that he stood to get a refund. Grinning, he said, "I'll find out how much next week!"

Another woman who talked to me—on the condition that I didn't use her name—said of the tax system, "I didn't know anything about it when I came here. I was told that you have to pay or they come after you and put you in jail or take your car." When I looked quizzically at Sadik Farah, he extended both of his hands in the woman's direction and shrugged his shoulders as if to say, "See what I mean?"

Outside the state apparatus, others worked to educate immigrants about taxes or other complicated aspects of government. At the African Development Center in Minneapolis—next to the KFAI Radio offices—Hussein Samatar put together business plans and handed out advice to entrepreneurs in the African diaspora. A poster of a Hiawatha light-rail car, in 1930s art deco, hung on the wall behind his desk, steaming full speed ahead. Another poster featured flags from every Latin American country—Samatar's hat tip to Minnesota's diversity.

Samatar played the role of middleman between immigrants and commercial banks or government lending agencies. Many Muslims refused to pay or receive interest because it violated more conservative interpretations of the Qur'an, a position that made it impossible for them to secure a traditional loan from a bank.

So Samatar patched things together. He secured start-up capital from banks and lending agencies, then lent the money to entrepreneurs, working out a deal that allowed them to pay him back with a return on his investment. No interest payments were involved, though it was only the means that changed, not the ends. Just like that, he said, snapping his fingers. "They love it. It makes sense."

Running a business in America was different, with paperwork and regulations that seemed overwhelming to many newcomers. But slowly people were adapting. "There are a lot of people who have been here three or four years or probably even longer, and they are uncomfortable," Samatar explained. "They are kind of feeling their way."

The snow was piled high on Riverside Avenue the morning Samatar and I met. I wore boots and a stocking cap as I negotiated the unplowed sidewalks leading to his office. But inside, Samatar relaxed in a red short-sleeve shirt and black wind pants. He hadn't been to Somalia in fifteen years and had no plans to return—at least not permanently. He had a wife, three children, a home in south Minneapolis, and a business that taught others like him how to make it. "Just like the Norwegians and the Swedes stayed, most of us will stay," he said with a laugh. "Moving on. Moving on."

Minnesotans thinking of Ethiopia are likely to remember the famines that have devastated the country for thirty years. The country has sixty-eight million people today. In 1973 alone, three hundred thousand peasants died from a lack of food and water. I remember reading about the country in junior high and seeing pictures of emaciated children with distended bellies.

When I started looking into the country's history—armed with little knowledge of it—I wondered, "What this time? What kind of chaotic, oppressive, undemocratic place did these folks come from?" Tracing the history of new Minnesotans was starting to feel like a broken record. It seemed like most of their native lands had a shared history: ruled by monarchs, then occupied by a Western power, then destroyed, after gaining their independence, by one pathetic despot or another. It seemed there was little hope for modernization in any of these places.

The real picture, of course, was complicated. Ethiopia shared many of the traits I was beginning to associate with third world and developing countries, but it was also a nation that had embarked on a grand democratic experiment after years of Marxism. (The country had been a cold war ally of the Soviet Union. For fourteen years, from 1977 to 1991, Mengistu Haile Mariam had ruled Ethiopia with an iron fist. His "Red Terror" campaign killed thousands of people, including many of the country's educated elite, in an attempt to quell dissent.) Elections in 2000 established the first popularly chosen government since the creation of the government of President Negasso Gidada and Prime Minister Meles Zenawi in 1995. The Ethiopian People's Revolutionary Democratic Front captured a vast majority of the parliamentary seats in that election and endorsed Zenawi as prime minister.

Those giant steps toward democracy made it all the more tragic that Ethiopia continued to succumb to the corruption and cronyism that infected much of Africa. The journalist Blaine Harden calls tribalism "the fundamental political illness of modern Africa." When I read that, I said it back to myself slowly. Fundamental . . . political . . . illness. That line, in a book Harden wrote called *Africa: Dispatches from a Fragile Continent,* caught my attention and made all the more sense in light of the conversations I had had with refugees and others about the closed nature of Ethiopian society— even after Ethiopians had come to America. The tendency to hide things was crippling.

Ethiopia also has the predictable substandard educational system, with a literacy rate of 35 percent. Women's living standards are meager. Female circumcision—a charitable phrase for what is known in human rights circles as female genital mutilation—remains a common practice. Many women must get permission from their husbands simply to go to the doctor.

After reading about the country's background, I wasn't hopeful for quick change among Ethiopians in Minnesota. The denial and ignorance that surrounded HIV/AIDS were rooted, as was the sympathy for polygamy in the Hmong community, in extreme devotion to the norms of tradition, religion, and patriarchy. Cultural ties were keeping many African immigrants from getting ahead. Change would come through shifting attitudes, community leadership, and political dialogue—but it would not come quickly or easily.

Ahmed Wassie was another Ethiopian doing his part to help the African immigrant community. He had lived in Minnesota a lot longer than most Africans. When he came to the Twin Cities in 1972, in fact, it was hard to find another person from his homeland. Wassie, too, worked in cramped quarters with meager resources, running a local radio program on KFAI that was sort of a rambling Q-and-A session. He was popular in the Ethiopian community and determined to break through the cultural taboos that he believed hampered progress among African immigrants.

Wassie wanted to devote airtime to the AIDS epidemic, but because of the sensitivity of the issue—

because the disease was basically a death sentence in Africa and because religious conservatism would surely keep people from tuning into any shows that dealt with sex—he couldn't come right out and tell people he was going to do a program about it. He had to lure them in with some other topic. So he would sometimes start off the monthly health segment of his show, *Voices of Ethiopia,* with a discussion of some common ailment like the flu or stomachaches. He would speak mostly in English and "sprinkle in a little Amharic," the official language of Ethiopia. Then he would pounce.

It was always dicey talking about sexually transmitted diseases. "I get a lot of calls whenever I mention AIDS. The majority are positive and people are glad I brought up the topic," he said. "But a couple of calls are really scary. They try to blame me for bringing up stories and say that I am dragging the good name of Ethiopia through the gutter. I say to them, 'Believe me. This is the [twenty-first] century, and AIDS is killing people. Denial has carried from Ethiopia to here.'"

Wassie said the difference between the cultures in the United States and Ethiopia was staggering. Like Somalis and the Hmong, Ethiopians have very close families, with loyalties skewed toward clans and their preferred religion (most Ethiopians are either Muslim, Christian, or animist), he said. That often led to dismissive attitudes toward shocking or different ideas and opinions. "We deny a lot of things," he said. "We just grew up that way. The society has a tendency to hide things, but I think we need to come out of that."

At times, I felt tempted to think of assimilation as a hopeless and unrealistic goal for new immigrants. Many of them were so different from the Minnesotans I had grown up with. The fight against HIV/AIDS seemed like one of those situations.

But health workers weren't throwing their hands in the air in frustration. In fact, there were many signs of hopeful progress. About forty people showed up at the Health Department's Minneapolis office for a meeting about the AIDS epidemic during the summer of 2002. That was a strong turnout, considering the touchiness of the subject. And there was always the hope that teenage immigrants were learning about AIDS prevention in the public schools.

Nearly a year after I wrote about the HIV/AIDS figures, the Health Department issued another report. Fresh cases had taken another jump among African immigrants. Nobody had expected the increase, and it was clear that it was still too early to tell whether a grassroots effort to get the word out about HIV/AIDS would change anything.

Tracy Sides was prepared for a long process, however, and said the agency would continue with its efforts to educate the community. As time went on, there

was hope for more involvement of immigrants themselves in educational campaigns. "One of the things we
are trying to do is collaborate and bring some African
communities together. It's very diverse, and we're still
collaborating and finding ways that would be effective,"
she told me. "We're still working with radio stations,
and as some of the people in the [immigrant] communities have become more mobile, we have had people in
those communities serve in that capacity, as well."

The Health Department hired an African woman to
serve as a liaison between the immigrant community
and the agency. The agency also recruited an Ethiopian
doctor to write columns about the HIV/AIDS epidemic
and other important health issues in an Amharic newspaper. It was timely: By 2004, the state demographer
estimated that as many as 7,500 Ethiopians were living
in Minnesota—not to mention many more Liberians,
Somalis, and other African refugees—and more were
on their way.

Gyuto Wheel of Dharma Monastery

A REALLY BIG CHANGE

A Mosque Comes to Minnesota

Zaid Khalid was right when he told me I might miss it. All I could see as I drove through the heart of Rochester were the ordinary restaurants and shops of Main Street Minnesota—nothing to suggest the sacred. Driving up and down Broadway Avenue a second time, I noticed a sign written in Arabic on a building with a stone facade. I was a little disappointed. The first mosque in southern Minnesota was in the hollowed-out guts of an American Legion hall.

Muslims had raised $200,000 to buy the hall in 1998, then passed the hat for another $600,000 in renovations. A big chunk of money—how much, they wouldn't say—came from a United Arab Emirates man who had been hospitalized at the Mayo Clinic. Praying in each others' basements or in rooms at the Kahler Hotel had grown stale, and the mosque was a hit. By 1998, Muslims were using it every day. They called it Masjid Abu Bakr Al-Sidique.

Islam was nothing new to Rochester. Highly educated Muslims from around the world had been living there for years, many of them doctors and engineers at the Mayo Clinic and IBM. But Islam remained on the margins of city life until Somalis began arriving from refugee camps or other parts of the far-flung diaspora. Refugees from the Balkan wars had also added to the Muslim population. Demographers estimated that there were 3,500 Muslims in the community by 2000—1,800 of them Somali; another 550, Bosnian.

It was a January day in 2002 when I visited. Stepping out of my car, I heard a deep and steady tenor wafting over the parking lot from within the walls of the building. The imam, the spiritual leader of the mosque, was summoning the men who were visiting outside. The shivering men, many without hats or gloves, moved into a warm entryway, took off their shoes, and shuffled in their socks into the worship area. The floor of the rectangular, whitewashed room was covered with a bright red carpet. I took off my shoes, followed the men inside, and, notebook and pen in hand, retreated to the back of the room.

The imam, covered in a white gown, chanted customary Arabic greetings. "God is Great. . . . There is no God except one God." About eighty men formed four rows behind the imam. Silently or praying softly, they fell to their knees, bowed with their faces to the ground, then got back to their feet—all the while facing east toward Mecca, the most important city in Islam.

Muslim identity was difficult to grasp. The Hispanics I encountered in small-town Minnesota had a shared Catholic faith with much of the population. The Russian expatriates I met were, like nearly everyone else in Minnesota, white. Even Asian immigrants seemed to fit in better than Muslims, perhaps because their Eastern religions were more difficult to understand and, consequently, of less interest.

Islam also carried a stigma after 9/11. In a *Minneapolis Star Tribune* poll more than two years after the attacks, 34 percent of Minnesotans said they believed Islam was more likely to promote violence in its believers than other religions (about half said Islam does not promote violence more than other religions). Three percent, meanwhile, said Christianity was more likely to promote violence than other religions, whereas 5 percent said the same thing about Judaisim and Buddhism. I hoped that by reporting on life at a Minnesota mosque, I could shed some light on the efforts of Muslims to create a positive public identity.

Rochester was a unique place for them—and the perfect location for an experiment in religious pluralism in Minnesota. The city had more racial or ethnic diversity than most parts of Minnesota outside of the Twin Cities.

The Mayo Clinic was one big reason; as many as three thousand patients from the Middle East alone were visiting the famed clinic every year, at least until 9/11, which temporarily curbed the visits of Arab aristocrats. (I once stayed at the Kahler Hotel when King Hussein of Jordan, not long before he died, was being treated for cancer. His entourage of aides and family members took up an entire floor of the hotel.) That exposure to diversity helped the city adapt when permanent changes in its ethnic and religious dimensions arrived.

There were signs of strife. Five years earlier, a twelve-year-old Somali boy lost eight teeth when men beat him with baseball bats. Two white men were convicted of assault and sent to prison, and some Somalis had been arrested after fights. A young African immigrant I met at the mosque said he rarely interacted with white students.

And there were acts of goodwill. The city waived parking meter enforcement near the mosque on Friday afternoons so that worshippers heading there from work could park for a few minutes near the mosque, say their prayers, and then leave without the hassle of feeding the meters. Police officers took cultural training courses. And the school district offered Muslim students the time and places to pray during the day.

"Really, if you compare what it was like in '95 to how it is now, you will see a tremendous difference," said Mohamoud Hamud, a counselor at the Mayo Clinic. He was philosophical about the cultural rifts and the pace of change. "We are all human beings, and we all have our inhibitions and baggage," Hamud said. "You can't expect someone to hug you in the spur of the moment. But this community is an integrated community."

Hamud was doing what he could to get involved. He took a seat on the school board in 2000 when he was chosen to complete the remaining nine months of the term of a board member who had moved out of state. Buoyed by the experience of community leadership, he ran, unsuccessfully, for a full term on the board in November 2001.

Zaid Khalid, the public face for the Islamic center, arranged my visit. He was excited about the flourishing of Islam in Rochester and wanted me—and anyone who might read my article—to know that. As he showed me around, he had a look about him that said, "Isn't this great?"

Khalid worked as a software engineer for IBM and had lived in Rochester for about five years. He spoke with me in the center's library, which was stocked with books and videos about Islam and spirituality, after I had observed the late-afternoon prayers. "We're glad to have you here," he told me more than once. Khalid talked about the difficulty of building a religious tradition in a city with few Muslims. Of his first few years in the city, he said, "It seemed like there were maybe thirty of us in the whole city. We had to meet for prayers in our basements."

I wondered about the differences between the educated Muslim elite—the physicians and engineers in town—and the working-class recent arrivals, such as Somalis. "With the coming of so many refugees, and all of them with their own cultures—many Somalis are from small villages and not educated very well in Islam—it caused some confusion among people who were not Muslim," Khalid said. "I think some of them are thinking, 'What is the culture of Islam?'"

Tenzin Chodak grabbed a pillow and knelt behind the shaded windows of an old house on Minnehaha Avenue in Minneapolis. The furniture that once filled the room had long been replaced by dusty throw rugs and flimsy bookshelves. Red and orange banners led to a sitting-room-turned-shrine, where a picture of the Dalai Lama hung next to a likeness of Buddha. Chodak was silent and peaceful, in the way of Tibetan Buddhists like himself.

The Gyuto Wheel of Dharma Monastery was the spiritual center for Tibetans who lived in Minnesota. The Tibetan refugee community was fifteen hundred strong; only New York had more. But the temple where they found their inspiration, where five monks lived and worshipped, could charitably be described as modest. Like the mosque in Rochester, it wasn't what I thought it would be.

Chodak, a cook at a suburban Twin Cities hospital, had come to worship a few days before the Dalai Lama planned to visit Minnesota. The Dalai Lama was set to speak in Minneapolis, and it was a chance Chodak couldn't miss. Blowing off the exiled spiritual leader of Tibetan Buddhists would be like a Catholic dissing the pope on one of his world tours. He wouldn't do it. Chodak's afternoon worship at the monastery was less than regular—he didn't come as often as he should, he admitted—but he would show up to see his spiritual guide.

Chodak wore a Minnesota Twins cap. Besides enjoying baseball, the TC stitched into the cap matched his initials. And it tied his identity, in a fun way, to his new home in the Upper Midwest. "Minnesota has been a good place to live. I like all of the religions here," he said, smiling and reminding me of the Buddhist tradition of free inquiry and tolerance for all beliefs. "Christian, Muslim, Hindu, whatever, it's no problem for me."

Nima Lhamo knelt next to Chodak, her husband, as the two visited with me. They had moved from India in the early 1990s when the United States was resettling Tibetans, and they clung to their faith amid Minnesota's sea of Lutherans and Catholics. They visited the monastery once a week.

The Dalai Lama had visited Minnesota five years earlier, on a trip that drew packed houses to Williams Arena
and Northrop Auditorium on the University of Minnesota campus in Minneapolis. He had also spoken to the
legislature. Now, His Holiness (as other Buddhists called
him) was returning for a checkup at the Mayo Clinic in
Rochester. His first stop would be in Minneapolis for
a speech at the city's convention center—an event, one
man at the monastery claimed, that would draw 99 percent of the Tibetans in Minnesota. "Not many will miss
this," he said, shaking his head. "Not many."

Tibetans needed a shot in the arm. Their community
was growing, but they were tucked into the nooks and
crannies of the Twin Cities, far from home in both geog-
raphy and ways of life. The connecting point, for many,
was the temple. But the one on Minnehaha Avenue—
like the one before it in New Brighton, a bit north of
Minneapolis—had become permanent when it was sup-
posed to be temporary.

"Tibetans are having a hard time without a permanent place to worship," said Lhamo, who worked as a
dialysis technician in the Twin Cities. A few years earlier, the actress Jessica Lange and her playwright husband Sam Shepard, who lived together in Minnesota
then, had headlined a fund-raiser that netted $50,000
in seed money for a new monastery. But in the spring
of 2006, it would still be months, maybe years, before
Tibetans actually had a better place to worship. In his

first visit, which I covered for the AP, the Dalai Lama raised thousands of dollars for the creation of a Tibetan cultural center in St. Paul.

This time, he wasn't raising money. But maybe his presence alone would draw attention to the local Tibetans' cause. Until then, they persevered. But the turquoise-sided house was a far cry from a faithful Buddhists' dreams. "At times, I want the people from *Extreme Makeover* to come here and fix it up!" Lhamo said.

"You better not print that," she said, hiding her face in her hands, surprised at her outburst. "We are grateful for what we have."

When the war in Iraq started, the mosques in Minnesota morphed from quiet spiritual centers into raucous town halls. They were the one place Muslims could go to exchange unvarnished opinions. I went to one in the northern Twin Cities suburb of Fridley the night the invasion began, looking for Muslim reaction to the war. But I also wondered how the war and its aftermath would affect the long-term relationship between Christians, Jews, and Muslims in Minnesota. My visit that night was a case in point: While I was sure that many of the men at the mosque were suspicious of me and the Western press, I also wondered whether any of them held extreme religious or political views that put them in sympathy with America's critics. I couldn't deny there was some tension in the air.

Odeh Muhawesh, a Jordanian who lived in Plymouth, another Twin Cities suburban community, led the discussion that night. The mosque, in the basement of a strip mall, was a popular spot for Iraqis. Sadiq Alnabi, an Iraqi dissident who lived in Fridley, worked at a convenience store, and had passionate views about the war, had invited me.

Many of the men were eager to return home if the invasion was a success, while others expressed reservations about the United States' intervention there. (One man, who identified himself as a Palestinian but wouldn't give me his name, told me he loved Minnesota but hated the United States' support for Israel. He wanted to know what I thought about Jewish settlements in the West Bank. I wasn't about to go down that precarious path, so I politely changed the subject.)

Muhawesh gave the most important speech of the night (as far as I could tell, that is; much of what he said, as was the case in many of my visits to mosques, had to be relayed to me through people willing to interpret). He told the men that if they ever returned to Iraq, they needed to promote the democratic values they had learned in America and in the mosques that stood side by side with churches and temples.

Those values were allowing them to meet freely that very night, he told them, in a religious setting of their choosing that was far removed from the religious mainstream in Minnesota. Speaking to the group of about twenty people, he told them to remember the important lessons they had learned in Minnesota and elsewhere in the United States—lessons about religious and ethnic diversity, openness, and free markets. He was sharply dressed and soft spoken. "I told them that they have had success in this free society, success with their businesses and in other areas," he said later when I asked him what he had talked about, "and that they must bring that with them."

Several men met with me after prayers at Rochester's Abu-Bakr Al-Sidique. They were thrilled to have a permanent place to worship—a place that helped them carve out an identity in mostly white, Christian southeastern Minnesota. "It's amazing that we have this mosque, and it's really been a big change," Mohammed Monirul Islam said. The twenty-seven-year-old was a bearded, soft-spoken IBM computer engineer from Bangladesh. Smiling, he added, "I feel great to see this change."

The worshippers were diverse. One Mayo Clinic physician in white chinos spoke better English than I did. An old man in a dirty coat, meanwhile, spoke no English and avoided me when I approached. A twelve-year-old boy sported a Minnesota Vikings jacket. It was evident that the highly educated Muslims who practiced a quiet form of Islam were joining with a larger group that included many Somalis and other newcomers.

Khalid introduced me to Amer Mikati, a forty-two-year-old pharmacist from Lebanon. He talked about the importance of daily community gatherings. I asked him if he felt any intolerance in the community. He said no. He was just excited about the mosque. "This is absolutely essential. Definitely. Gathering together is part of every community. This is our center of community gathering." The imam, too, said, "Islam wants you to be sociable."

Somalis made up many of the newest Muslim immigrants. The state agency Minnesota Planning said the Rochester School District had 462 Somali-speaking students in 2000. That compared with 1,553 in the Minneapolis district, 131 in Owatonna, 87 in St. Paul, and 59 in Mankato.

Several Somalis I spoke with said they had learned about Rochester in refugee camps and were told it was a safe and tolerant place with good schools and abundant jobs. That included seventeen-year-old Ahmed Abdullah, who was organizing videos and audiotapes in the library of the Islamic center. He looked like a serious young man in his flat, multicolored hat, the kind I had seen on many black and Muslim activists on television (the football great Jim Brown came to mind). Abdullah said the center provided some refuge for him and others bound by Islamic traditions.

He acknowledged there were tensions between some students. "You come to America, and people don't understand your point of view. You always have to work it out between points of view," he said. He said he helped with a conflict resolution group at Mayo High School and enjoyed his classes and classmates. When I asked him if he ever hung out with white kids, he paused and smiled. "I participate with the American-born kids in school, but otherwise there's not a lot of socializing. But it's terrific here. I really enjoy the education I'm getting. It's terrific—except for the cold."

Khalid wanted to talk for another minute before I left and summoned me to the table where he was sitting. He had a round face and a thick beard and wore a gray sweater. With his slightly disheveled look and serious manner, he reminded me of a graduate student. Khalid wanted me to know that the library in the Islamic center was open all day once a month, so anyone from town could come for a visit. Arab videos and movies—some religious, some secular—lined the shelves. The center hosted some community education classes. Here's a Qur'an, he said. Take it with you. Everybody was welcome in this new and different world.

Joselyn and Christino Casarez

WE ARE HERE

Hispanics Shape an Identity

Angel Morales wasn't sure what to think about the hip-hop dress favored by Hispanics at his son's suburban high school. To him, it was another sign of how American culture overwhelmed the identity of immigrant youth. He flicked a business card with his finger, trying to find the right words. "I guess nobody remembers where they come from anymore," he said. For Morales, there was no doubt. If he hadn't said so, his thick shock of black hair, thin mustache, and cowboy boots would have given it away. He was Mexican at his roots, and proud of it.

Morales left Mexico for the United States in the early 1990s. He went to California with his family first before trading in factory work for life as a community organizer in the Midwest. He loved living in the Twin Cities, and at the same time he never forgot about home. But he didn't think the children of his generation knew much about their heritage or—even more discouraging—

what their parents or grandparents had gone through to come to America and build a decent life. He hoped to change that.

I met Morales at the Resource Center of the Americas, a community action center with a café near Lake Street in Minneapolis. Many immigrants hung out at the café for the camaraderie, the Latin American food, and the fair-trade coffee it served. But its main function was to organize around the principles of social justice—often with a leftist bent. Its library shelves were lined with books by the radical MIT professor Noam Chomsky and other intellectuals who were critical of free trade and American influence in Latin America.

Morales had served with the Institute for Mexicans Abroad, an organization created by President Vicente Fox to help Mexicans living in the diaspora. When we met during the winter of 2006, he had just returned from Mexico, where he had registered to vote in that country's upcoming presidential election. He was encouraging other Mexicans living in Minnesota to return home to register, as well, arguing that they had a stake in their native country's future. More than 5,000 planned to cast ballots.

He was also the project director for a community development organization called Latinos en Acción, but his current initiative was Casa Mexico, or Mexico House. Morales and some other parents had founded the organization as a way to promote Latin American culture among the estimated 175,000 Hispanics living in Minnesota. Casa Mexico was organizing neighborhood soccer leagues, helping students travel to see their grandparents in Latin America, and doling out advice to immigrants who wanted to buy houses back home. Mexicans, Guatemalans, Salvadorans, Colombians, and Ecuadorians had already joined the group.

Morales handed me the business card. To the left of the words "Casa Mexico" was a green image of Minnesota. Inside the state, there was a red image of Mexico above a gray sketch of an ancient pyramid. His identities, I thought, all wrapped into one.

"Some people have said to me, 'Are you trying to divide people?'" he said, shrugging his shoulders. "Of course, that is not what this is about." The politics of the center weren't for Morales. Rather, he wanted people to get involved in things Hispanic immigrants could all agree about. "There are times when a political issue comes up, and people are asked to speak up or participate, and then nothing happens. But these cultural things, or sports—people respond to that more," he explained. He hoped to rally Latin Americans around common interests, creating Minnesotans who kept the uniqueness of their heritage alive.

"When you have an identity, you are healthy, and this is a way to get in touch with that," Atzin Ketter said. Ketter had just finished dancing with a dozen others in the middle of Me Gusta, a Mexican restaurant on Lake Street in Minneapolis. The dancers—some in headdresses and beating drums—stomped their feet, spun, and chanted. Morales had invited Danza Mexica Cuauhtemoc to kick off an evening devoted to his new organization. It was a good show, and the crowd loved it. But I wondered what native dancing had to do with twenty-first-century immigrants in Minnesota.

"Everyone needs an identity, to know who they really are," said Ketter, who was Mexican on her father's side. "Probably there are a lot of young people who live in this country and don't know much about their culture. There's a gang influence here, and I want to help keep kids away from that. Maybe this kind of thing—dancing or whatever cultural things we might do—maybe they draw attention to something else, something larger."

The sweat soaked through the red bandana wrapped around Betto Limón's head. He wore earrings, a thick beaded necklace, and white pants and shirt for the dance routine. An artist, Limón had grown up in Mexico City before coming to Minnesota. He had lived in Northfield before moving to the Twin Cities suburb of Lakeville, doing odd construction jobs to pay the bills. "When I come here, I feel more into my culture," he said, gesturing to the rest of the dance troupe. He said he mostly hung around other immigrants, though he'd been in Minnesota for about five years.

Limón was glad Morales had started Casa Mexico and

planned to take part in other events. When I asked him if he considered himself to be Mexican or American, he smiled at the question. "Of course, I am 100 percent Mexican!" he replied. But he also said he didn't plan to return to Mexico any time soon—if ever. Why wouldn't he, I asked him, if he remained so devoted to Mexico while living in the United States? "I don't know. It's just who I am, and that never changes," he said. "But I like it here, too."

According to the World Bank, Mexico is the most prosperous of all the Latin American countries, with a per capita income of $6,770 in 2004. It had an emerging middle class, a president who had been chosen from a party outside the long ruling Institutional Revolutionary Party for the first time since 1929, and a *Freedom House* ranking of free. But it was still overwhelmingly poor. Half of all Mexicans lived in poverty while nearly half of the country's wealth was in the hands of an oligarchy that made up 10 percent of the population. Workers continued to pour across Mexico's northern border into the United States—many of them finding their way to the Midwest and into Minnesota.

In the heated debate over immigration—which picked up steam in the spring of 2006, when Congress began rolling out plans for tightening the nation's immigration policy—conventional wisdom put the number of illegal immigrants in the United States at 12 million.

But nobody really knew how many were here. When I covered an immigrant rally in Minneapolis in the midst of the congressional debate, my editor asked me to find out whether the people I was interviewing held legal residency. I tried for a while to find out, but asking was pointless. Nobody was going to tell me they were in the country illegally as I stood there with a pen and notebook in hand, ready to write down their name and immigration status. I knew there were illegal immigrants in the crowd who might one day be sent home, but the more important questions were why they were here, and what they planned to do now.

In the case of Minnesota's refugees, there was little question about legality. The Hmong and Somalis, for instance, were political refugees who had been granted asylum by the United States. The vast majority had legal status and had entered the country legally after long journeys from Africa or Asia. But for many Hispanic immigrants, their journey to Minnesota had begun with an illegal trek across the southern border, for better lives that remained mostly hidden from Minnesotans.

Cultural preservation was deeply woven into many immigrant organizations. Hmong groups, for instance, have for years held a tournament in St. Paul where Hmong youth compete in soccer and such native activities as kato, a game in which a ball is kicked back and forth over a net. But retaining those cultural ties was often a more subtle process, especially in the smaller towns where immigrant or refugee fraternal groups held less sway.

In May of 2006, I traveled on assignment to southwestern Minnesota, where, in the heart of the state's farm country, the Hispanic population had reached 20 percent in some towns. Food-processing plants and other labor-intensive industries provided most of the employment, but by then there were also many immigrant entrepreneurs, and I wanted to meet them.

Behind the dusty brick facades of old Main Streets, immigrants were quietly running restaurants, clothing stores, barbershops, and translation services—helping to breathe new life into downtowns that had been in decline for decades. Downtown property was cheaper than it was in newer commercial districts, more readily available, and often located near low-income housing. For many newcomers, it was the first step toward the American dream.

Maria Parga ran a clothing store in downtown Worthington, selling dresses for weddings and First Communions, soccer uniforms and other clothing for the city's growing Hispanic community. She had come to Worthington in the early 1990s, long before there was much of a Hispanic presence there, and opened a general store where she sold groceries and rented videos, mostly to other Hispanics.

Parga's clothing store near Lake Okabena was one of a half-dozen downtown shops immigrants had opened in the past two or three years in the city's once-bustling commercial core. We met in front of the store on a hot May afternoon. Parga's daughter, Elizabeth Flores, was the subject of a graduation feature in that day's *Daily Globe,* her picture visible through the window of the newspaper stand nearby. Despite being married and caring for a young child, Flores had finished high school. Parga, known as a workaholic who put in ten to twelve hours a day running her stores, said with a smile, "She's worked very hard for her diploma."

The store was quiet, with a few Hispanic customers looking for some summer clothing. "I just saw a need for another place for people to find stuff," Parga said, "and this is a good location, at the center of town. We like it here." An elderly white man carrying a grocery bag stopped in and offered Parga and her sister, Luisa Rodriguez, some fresh rhubarb. The women threw puzzled looks at each other, and Parga told him with a laugh, "We don't know what to do with that!" He gave them a mock surprised look, eyes wide open: "You mean you haven't had strawberry-rhubarb pie?" he asked. "It's the best."

Parga thanked him as he walked out, then said to me, "We have a different culture, and we are serving a niche. Sometimes there are white customers who come in like just now, but not very often. I would like to have more of that." Still, the shop offered the chance for small connections in a city that was still adjusting to newcomers years after they had first arrived.

"These new shops have helped provide interest in downtown again," the city's community development director, Brad Chapulis, told me. "That's no easy feat, because as you know these downtowns have struggled for a long time." At least some of the city's 25 percent growth in commercial property taxes over five years could be credited to immigrant entrepreneurs.

Adolfo Avila sensed history when he looked at the old buildings and facades lining rural Main Streets, many of them a century old or more. He also saw a future for immigrants in the Upper Midwest.

Avila sat in front of a five-foot-long American flag tacked to his office wall. He ran a translation service and helped other Hispanic entrepreneurs get the help they needed to start businesses in the small towns around Marshall. "They have all these old buildings that other people that already have money are not worried about. They don't want them," said Avila, who had grown up in Texas and whose parents were from Mexico. "And then you got people that come along that don't have anything and are willing to put money in it and fix it up and make it a business. It's a win-win situation."

Avila, who had served in Desert Storm, had moved to Minnesota four-and-a-half years earlier with his wife and four children. Not long after he arrived, entrepreneurs began calling and asking him how to get started. They didn't know where to go for advice or start-up capital. "There was a real need for a Spanish-speaking consultant to help people navigate all of this," he said. "There was no trust."

So while some immigrants were trying to reclaim their identity, others were forming new ones. In the farm country of southwestern Minnesota, where immigrant entrepreneurs strove to make it in the heart of Americana, it was a little of both.

In the spring of 2006, President Bush proposed a bill to create a guest worker program for illegal immigrants while also offering many a path toward citizenship. The House of Representatives had already passed legislation to toughen border security while making illegal immigrants subject to felony charges. The Senate, meanwhile, backed tougher border enforcement while also backing, like Bush, avenues to obtain citizenship. Public polling showed overwhelming opposition to the felony provision but strong support for tighter borders. It was a mishmash of ideas, with no clear consensus in sight.

In the midst of the debate, on an April afternoon, some thirty thousand people showed up on the grounds of the Minnesota Capitol in response to the get-tough measures. The gathering was part of a web of immigrant rallies across the nation that drew the public's sympathy. But a few weeks later, when activists called on immi-

grants to shutter their businesses, walk off the job, and
skip school—as a way to show their importance to the
American economy—the idea got a different response
among many immigrants and the public.

Many businesses did indeed close their doors during
the May 1 walkout. The Mercado Market on Lake Street
in Minneapolis shuttered its forty stores, restaurants,
and shops. Swift & Co. closed its meat-processing plant
in Worthington. Forty-five percent of the Hispanic high
school students skipped class in St. James, and there were
higher-than-usual Hispanic student absences in places
like Willmar.

"We are just here trying to help people, to fight for
something," said Guillermo Ordaz, who had come to a
rally at Powderhorn Park in Minneapolis with his girl-
friend, Cecilia Aguero. Pausing to find the right words,
he added, "Equality. That's what this is about. Equality."

Ordaz, who worked at a Ruby Tuesday restaurant in
Plymouth, hailed from Mexico while Aguero had come
to the United States from Peru. The two stood side by
side with their arms around each other as speakers
whipped up the crowd. "We are here working, but people
treat us like criminals," Aguero said. "And of course, if we
have to leave, how will we ever be together?"

But for the most part, it seemed like business as usual.
The Jennie-O Turkey Store kept its plants open in Willmar and Melrose and reported nothing unusual in absences. At the Hyatt Regency, a plush hotel in downtown

Minneapolis whose workers represented more than thirty nationalities, nearly everyone showed up for work. Few students joined rallies and teach-ins at Macalester College and the College of St. Catherine in St. Paul. And the rally at Powderhorn Park drew perhaps a thousand people—far fewer than the Capitol rally of a month before. American flags flew next to Mexican ones, and the leaders at the rally exhorted those gathered to call their representatives in Congress and to write letters to the editor. Subsequent polls showed that the public had less tolerance for the May 1 boycott than the earlier April rallies. It was a day of sweeping rhetoric—but fewer people seemed to be listening.

Sophia Gonzalez, who managed a clothing shop in the Mercado Market on Lake Street, had a simple answer for me: "It's a bad idea. We have to keep the jobs, because we need the work." The market was part of a stretch of Lake Street that had 250 Hispanic-owned shops. It was the crown jewel of immigrant economic development in Minnesota—there had been just four immigrant-owned shops in the same area in 1992. Now here it was, shutting down for an entire business day. Gonzalez was angry. She was thirty-five, had grown up in Mexico, and was glad to have a job in a Mexican market with familiar surroundings. "We need to follow the rules, in America, because we live here. No work or school is not a good idea," she said.

Alex Perez was a Minneapolis security guard with

dreams of selling real estate. He didn't think much of
the boycott, either. To him, it went against Hispanics'
hard-won reputation as good workers. The boycott could
backfire with the public and, worse, reverse the goodwill that had developed during the rallies held a few
weeks before. "If I am scheduled to work, I will work,"
said Perez, who was from Mexico. "A lot of people come
to this country to work hard, because it's hard to earn
money in Mexico. I have to work and pay the mortgage,
anyway, so I will go to work."

Even so, Perez sympathized with the reasons behind the boycott. He understood the message that immigrants were trying to send to the country—and to
the state of Minnesota. He wasn't going to take part,
and he knew the walkout would send mixed signals to
Minnesotans about immigrant allegiance. The boycott,
however, was a plea for acceptance and recognition, if a
clumsy and misunderstood one. As Perez put it, "It's a
way to say, 'We are here,' you know?"

EPILOGUE

I was a few months short of five in the summer of 1973, when *Time* magazine ran a story that honed Minnesota's reputation for clean politics, good schools, environmental conservation—and remarkable homogeneity. Governor Wendell Anderson, in khakis and a plaid shirt, smiles proudly on the magazine's cover as he shows off a lanky northern pike on a stringer. The caption reads, "The Good life in Minnesota." The good life, according to the article, included a "comparatively serene and open population." But with the state's largest minority group, African Americans, making up just 1 percent of the population—and the new migration years away—the magazine concluded that Minnesota lacked "the fire, urgency and self-accusation of states with massive urban centers and problems."

That article and the iconic Anderson photograph helped to shape modern Minnesota's reputation. Yet reading it now is to return to an era long past. In 1973, whites made up 98 percent of the state's population; today, that figure has dropped to 88 percent. Relaxed entry requirements for Africans, a growing market for unskilled labor in rural areas—which also draws illegal immigrants—and the recruitment of high-tech workers in the Twin Cities promise to alter the population even more. There will be many more stories of immigrants and refugees.

As this book has tried to show, these newcomers often struggle over issues of culture and heritage, but much of that tension stems from the understandable and age-old conflicts between generations. Some of those old ways—as they pass through the cultural strainer—won't last in a new land. That may well be a part of the crucial "fire, urgency and self-accusation" that *Time* found missing from Minnesota long ago.

The immigrants who built Minnesota long ago were outsiders who eventually found a place in society. One of my great-grandmothers, as the story goes, changed her Swedish name upon arriving in the United States to make it sound more "American." That reminded me of a Hmong man I once met named Chong who preferred to be called "Bob"—a most American name if there ever was one. So I take the long view in considering the immigrant experience.

Historian Carlton Qualey, recounted Theodore Blegen in *Minnesota: A History of the State,* found evidence of

Minnesota's early immigrant influence in choral music, food preparation, idiomatic speech and writing, immigrant literature, and "the strong belief of all groups in the benefits of the American way of life." Qualey believed that, over time, what remains of the immigrant experience is recognized and appreciated through such stable institutions as churches, schools, and social organizations. Blegen agreed: "From the era of the French to contemporary times," he writes, "Minnesota owes much of its distinctive character as a commonwealth to its cultural ties with the New and Old Worlds that brought vigor and talent to the task of building a modern state in what was once a wilderness." What might one day be said of new immigrants and their influences?

The stories in this book are also about new people not simply fitting in and accepting change, but doing so in a way that protects what is unique and meaningful about their lives. That is the trick of assimilation. A published compilation of essays and poems written by Hmong authors, *Bamboo among the Oaks: Contemporary Writing by Hmong Americans,* is all about this particular and important crisis of identity. One of the authors, Pa Xiong, writes about the tension in her traditional home in a poem called "The Green House":

> . . . I cannot leave this green house
> they say the world outside these wooden doors is
> bad

in this green house
they say I must be Hmong
and I am
without understanding what they mean
they close their eyes when I undress myself
they are deaf when I speak
they clothe me in the old ways that I cannot
     understand
traditions that have become too heavy
I have worn them on my back for too long
as woman and as child
I know I cannot stay
buried voiceless
I returned home to the green house
only to remind myself why I left in the first place

My drive to work through south Minneapolis takes
me near a stretch of Lake Street that has shops cater-
ing to Latinos and Somalis and grocery stores run by
Ethiopians and Liberians. An American Indian center
has stood there for years, as well as the Scandinavian
shop popular for its lefse, Swedish meatballs, and other
Nordic treats. Trips into St. Paul sometimes lead me
past a Hmong neighborhood, a Somali fraternal organization, and a Kurdish restaurant run by a man
from Iraq. When I drive through rural Minnesota on
assignment for the AP, I sometimes see Hispanics toil-
ing in the fields. Somalis walk the downtown streets of

my hometown. And one of my wife's favorite teachers is a Russian immigrant who came to the United States with her husband and sons during the age of glasnost and perestroika. So it's not just our grandparents' Minnesota.

Maybe it never really was. The forces of history have been behind all of the great migrations to Minnesota. Europeans fled the uncertainties of the Industrial Revolution more than a century ago, followed by Eastern Europeans who escaped communism during the Cold War and, later, Vietnamese who sought refuge after a devastating war in their homeland. Likewise, most of the new Minnesotans have fled political or economic turmoil, leaving their old lives behind.

Minnesota has changed a lot since my first encounter with new immigrants, back when I was writing about a trailer park in Willmar. More than a decade later, immigrants and refugees have become a part of the fabric of many cities—competing in high school sports, running small businesses, taking part in religious congregations—rather than existing as curiosities.

But there are still tensions and unanswerable questions about how they will ultimately fit in. In meeting newcomers where they live and work, and watching their interaction with the Minnesotans around them, I sense a mixture of isolation, struggle, and hope.

On a recent trip through rural Minnesota, I met Ahmed Omar, a young Somali man, at the Marshall store where he ran the till and stocked the shelves. Hindi Quality Cultural Products sat just off the street that ran through the heart of downtown. It had an alleyway entrance and a tiny sign over the door, and it was empty except for Omar when I poked my head inside.

Omar moved to Minnesota in 1998 after years in a refugee camp in Kenya and a brief stay in Sioux Falls, South Dakota. He played basketball for Marshall High School and graduated in 2001. His wife, Sadia Salah, was also a graduate of the local high school, and the two decided to make the city of about 13,000 their permanent home. They dreamed of starting a store.

With Omar's savings and a loan from his father, the couple opened the store in 2005 and also rented the apartment above it. They weren't making great money, but they were getting by. Life in small-town Minnesota could be a little isolating for a family from Africa, but it wasn't too bad. The people were nice. I asked the twenty-five-year-old Omar what the future held for someone his age. Was life in the American Midwest a good long-term fit for him and his family, or was a return to Somalia possible?

"You know, it's going to take another ten years to fix that country. So there's no going back," he said. "For us, Minnesota is home." They were, like the rest of the state, moving ahead.

ACKNOWLEDGMENTS

My journalism career began around the time new immigrants and refugees were coming to Minnesota. So it was luck, in many ways, that gave me the chance to explore this subject. But several editors also encouraged me to write about these newcomers.

Dave Pyle and Doug Glass, the AP's Minneapolis bureau chief and news editor, respectively, urged me to write about the Somalis, Ethiopians, and others now living in Minnesota. Forrest Peterson, who as editor of the *West Central Tribune* gave me my first job in jour nalism, put me onto stories about Hispanic migration and Soviet expatriates living in rural Minnesota. And Tom Hamburger, the Washington bureau chief for the *Minneapolis Star Tribune* the summer I worked there, assigned stories about the Hmong who were visiting the nation's capital.

At Syren Book Company, this project was greatly improved by the thoughtful work of my team of editors and designers: Maria Manske, Wendy Holdman, Mary Byers, and Kyle Hunter. Joel Wurl, in writing the foreword,

added an important perspective through his work study-
ing immigration at the University of Minnesota.

Several people read drafts of this work and offered
valuable insight, including my friend and AP colleague
Brian Bakst, a keen observer of Minnesota politics; my
friend Dave Aeikens, a reporter for the *St. Cloud Times*
and a student of the state's history; and my parents, Paul
and DeElla Aamot, who also contributed meaningfully
by passing down their interest in our family's heritage.
My wife, Jeanne, served as an editor and sounding board
and was a vessel of encouragement. More important, her
empathy helped me to better understand people from all
walks of life.

Finally, the scores of people who agreed to be in-
terviewed, offering their thoughts about the difficult
process of assimilation, made this book possible while
broadening my view of the human experience.

SOURCES

The most valuable sources of information for this book were personal interviews conducted in the course of my work as a reporter. The main chapters are largely based on articles I wrote for the Associated Press, supplemented by unpublished notes and further reporting. I also combed through reports I wrote for the *West Central Tribune,* the *Minneapolis Star Tribune,* and Minnesota-based magazines.

Furthermore, I learned a great deal by reading the work of others at the AP, the *Minneapolis Star Tribune,* the *St. Paul Pioneer Press,* the *Rochester Post-Bulletin,* and other newspapers in Minnesota. Books about Minnesota and the countries where the state's newest immigrants are from were essential in providing historical facts and perspective.

Here are the main sources for each section:

Author's Note: William E. Lass, *Minnesota: A History* (New York: W.W. Norton, 1977, 1983).

Introduction: William E. Lass, *Minnesota: A History* (New York: W.W. Norton, 1977, 1983); Theodore Blegen, *Minnesota: A History of the State* (Minneapolis: University of Minnesota Press, 1963, 1975); D. J. Tice, *Minnesota's Twentieth Century: Stories of Extraordinary Everyday People* (Minneapolis: University of Minnesota Press, in cooperation with the *St. Paul Pioneer Press,* 1999); Bill Holm, *The Heart Can Be Filled Anywhere on Earth* (Minneapolis: Milkweed Editions, 2000); Rhoda R. Gilman, *The Story of Minnesota's Past* (St. Paul: Minnesota Historical Society Press, 1989, 1991); Odd Lovoll, *The Promise of America: A History of the Norwegian-American People* (Minneapolis: University of Minnesota Press, in cooperation with the Norwegian-American Historical Association, 1984); Jon Gjerde and Carlton C. Qualey, *Norwegians in Minnesota: The People of Minnesota* (St. Paul: Minnesota Historical Society Press, 2002); Hyman Berman and Linda Mack Schloff, *Jews in Minnesota* (St. Paul: Minnesota Historical Society Press, 2002); Kathleen Neils Conzen, *Germans in Minnesota* (St. Paul: Minnesota Historical Society Press, 2003); *American Immigrant Cultures: Builders of a Nation,* 2 vols. (New York: Simon & Schuster, 1997); Steven J. Keillor, *Hjalmar Petersen of Minnesota: The Politics of Provincial Independence* (St. Paul: Minnesota Historical Society Press, 1987); "Bridging the Gap between Community and Hispanic Immigrants," *Minnesota Cities* (November 1994); "Neighborhood under Siege," *West Central Tribune* (Aug. 22,

1994); "Russian Couple Enjoys First Christmas in Willmar," *West Central Tribune* (Dec. 28, 1992); "Bulgarian Is Eager to Control His Future in the United States," *West Central Tribune* (Aug. 7, 1993); "'I'm doing this for my family,'" *West Central Tribune* (April 7, 1995); "Having Left the Iron Curtain Behind, Two Willmarites Eye Yeltsin Power Struggle," *West Central Tribune* (April 9, 1993); "Elm Lane Owner Fails to Meet Deadline," *West Central Tribune* (July 1, 1994); "Landlord Target of Probe," *West Central Tribune* (June 25, 1994); "Elm Lane Owner Fined $15,000," *West Central Tribune* (Oct. 27, 1994).

An Ongoing Problem: Adrian Karatnycky (ed.), *Freedom in the World: The Annual Survey of Political Rights and Civil Liberties* (Lanham, Md.: Rowman & Littlefield, 2003); "Hmong Grapple with Lingering Effects of Polygamy," Associated Press (Nov. 15, 2002); Mai Neng Moua (ed.), *Bamboo among the Oaks: Contemporary Writing by Hmong Americans* (St. Paul: Minnesota Historical Society Press, 2002); "Hmong Search for Site for Traditional Funerals," Associated Press (Feb. 16, 2003); Sucheng Chan, *Hmong Means Free: Life in Laos and America* (Philadelphia: Temple University Press, 1994).

Out There by Ourselves: "Vanguard of a new wave of Hmong refugees arrives in Minnesota," Associated Press (June 21, 2004); "Minnesota's Hmong, Once Refugees Themselves, Ready to Embrace New Wave," Associated

Press (Jan. 25, 2004); "Hmong Go to Capitol to Protest Pending U.S. Trade with Laos," *Minneapolis Star Tribune* (July 16, 1997); "Hmong Putting American Politics to Work for Them," *Minneapolis Star Tribune* (Aug. 18, 1997); "Hmong Veterans Back Vento Bill," *Minneapolis Star Tribune* (June 27, 1997); "Improved Trade Status for Laos Hits Obstacles in Congress," *Minneapolis Star Tribune* (July 25, 1997); "Mayor Visits Hmong Refugees Ahead of Resettlement in Minnesota," Associated Press (March 2, 2004).

Them against Us: Adrian Karatnycky (ed.), *Freedom in the World: The Annual Survey of Political Rights and Civil Liberties* (Lanham, Md.: Rowman & Littlefield, 2003); Mark Bowden, *Black Hawk Down: A Story of Modern War* (New York: Atlantic Monthly Press, 1999); Salome C. Nnoromele, *Somalia* (San Diego: Lucent Books, 2000); "Minnesota's Somalis Find Their Voice, and It's an Angry One," Associated Press (March 22, 2002); "Somali Leaders Call for Full Investigation of Police Shooting," Associated Press (March 11, 2002).

A Most Urgent Matter: Adrian Karatnycky (ed.), *Freedom in the World: The Annual Survey of Political Rights and Civil Liberties* (Lanham, Md.: Rowman & Littlefield, 2003); "Edwards Talks Jobs and Trade in Minnesota Visit," Associated Press (Feb. 21, 2004); "Far from Home, Somalis Press U.S. to Aid Emerging Government," Associated Press (Sept. 25, 2005); "Far Away in

Exile, Refugees Keep Up the Heat from Minnesota," Associated Press (Jan. 29, 2006).

Living in Denial: Adrian Karatnycky (ed.), *Freedom in the World: The Annual Survey of Political Rights and Civil Liberties* (Lanham, Md.: Rowman & Littlefield, 2003); Blaine Harden, *Africa: Dispatches from a Fragile Continent* (New York: W.W. Norton, 1990); Laurel Corona, *Ethiopia* (San Diego: Lucent Books, 2001); "Denial, Stigma Hinder State Effort against AIDS in Immigrants," Associated Press (July 26, 2002); "Somali Tax Preparers Investigated by State, IRS," Associated Press (May 21, 2004); "Somalis: Tax Fraud Teaching Community Lesson on Tax System," Associated Press (May 22, 2004); "More AIDS Awareness Funding Sought for African-born Residents," Associated Press (Feb. 8, 2005); "States, Uncle Sam Delicately Bring New Immigrants into Tax System," Associated Press (April 12, 2006).

A Really Big Change: "Mosque Helps Rochester's Muslims Stake Claim to Their New Home," Associated Press (Feb. 2, 2001); "Thousands Flock to Hear Dalai Lama's Wisdom," Associated Press (May 8, 2001); "Dalai Lama Brings Message of Peace to Legislature," Associated Press (May 9, 2001); "Jessica Lange, Sam Shepard Playing Host to Benefit for Local Buddhist Monastery," Associated Press (Nov. 5, 2001); "Iraqis in Minnesota Can See It Now: A Democratic Iraq," Associated Press (April 9, 2003); "Minnesota Iraqis Consider Going

Home," Associated Press (April 10, 2003); "Minnesota Tibetans Hope for a Boost from Dalai Lama Visit," Associated Press (April 13, 2006); "Minnesota Poll: Most Say Religion has Role in World's Conflicts," *Minneapolis Star Tribune* (Dec. 28, 2003).

We Are Here: Adrian Karatnycky (ed.), *Freedom in the World: The Annual Survey of Political Rights and Civil Liberties* (Lanham, Md.: Rowman & Littlefield, 2003); World Bank, www.worldbank.org; "Workers, Students Walk Out on 'Day without Immigrants,'" Associated Press (May 1, 2006); "Boycotting the Boycott? Immigrants Ponder May 1 Walkout," Associated Press (April 29, 2006); "Midwest Immigrants Finding American Dream on Old Main Street," Associated Press (June 17, 2006).

Epilogue: "Minnesota: A State That Works," *Time* (Aug. 13, 1973); Theodore Blegen, *Minnesota: A History of the State* (Minneapolis: University of Minnesota Press, 1963, 1975); Mai Neng Moua (ed.), *Bamboo among the Oaks: Contemporary Writing by Hmong Americans* (St. Paul: Minnesota Historical Society Press, 2002); David Vassar Taylor, *African Americans in Minnesota* (St. Paul: Minnesota Historical Society Press, 2002); June Drenning Holmquist (ed.), *They Chose Minnesota* (St. Paul: Minnesota Historical Society Press, 1981); Robert Putnam, *Bowling Alone: The Collapse and Revival of American Community* (New York: Simon & Schuster, 2000).

To order additional copies of *The New Minnesotans*:

Web: www.itascabooks.com

Phone: 1-800-901-3480

Fax: Copy and fill out the form below with credit card information. Fax to 763-398-0198.

Mail: Copy and fill out the form below. Mail with check or credit card information to:

Syren Book Company
5120 Cedar Lake Road
Minneapolis, Minnesota 55416

Order Form

Copies	Title / Author	Price	Totals	
	The New Minnesotans / Gregg Aamot	$14.95	$	
	Subtotal		$	
	7% sales tax (MN only)		$	
	Shipping and handling, first copy		$	4.00
	Shipping and handling, ___ add'l copies @$1.00 ea.		$	
	TOTAL TO REMIT		$	

Payment Information:

__ Check Enclosed __ Visa/MasterCard		
Card number:	Expiration date:	
Name on card:		
Billing address:		
City:	State:	Zip:
Signature :	Date:	

Shipping Information:

__ Same as billing address __ Other (enter below)		
Name:		
Address:		
City:	State:	Zip: